UNFORGIVING
Strategise. Dominate. Conquer.

AKASH BENALI

INDIA · SINGAPORE · MALAYSIA

ISBN
Paperback 979-8-89632-400-3
Hardcase 979-8-89673-751-3

Contents

Contents

Acknowledgements

I would like to start by thanking my parents for raising me the way they did. I would also like to thank them for teaching me things the hard way and instilling core values that I still believe in and follow to this day.

A special shout out to my mother for holding the fort in our tough times. She never expressed it, but she didn't want me to pursue a career in sports, knowing its unpredictable nature. Yet she has supported me for the past 20 years and, to this date, by waking up early to look after my nutrition and to make sure I have everything ready when it comes to playing a match or practising, all along while also looking after the house. She made sure she kept me grounded by speaking the truth and reminding me that life can be unpredictable. I can never thank her enough.

To my sister for inspiring me by being such a tough cookie herself and making sure that the family sees through the tough period. Special thanks to her for bringing an angel, my niece, into this world and our lives. Thank you for giving our family a reason to smile. It came as an opportunity for me to stay motivated, and for her, I decided to continue my journey as an athlete. Without my sister, my family's life would have been harder, and we would not have been where we are today.

To my closest friends, brothers & schoolmates, Major Akash Pawar and Adv Pratik Tendulkar, for inspiring me and being with me at every step of my sporting and entrepreneurial career, Thank you.

A heartfelt thank you to Darshan and Amit for being my pillars of support and always saying yes to everything I've asked of them.

A big thank you to everyone in the cricketing fraternity who supported me, and an even bigger thank you to those who didn't. Your challenges taught me invaluable lessons that I would never have learnt otherwise. These lessons have shaped this book, enabling me to share insights with parents and athletes to make their journey on the field a little easier.

A heartfelt thank you to all my ever-enthusiastic and supportive gym members. While your role may have seemed small, you've been an integral part of my cricket journey, witnessing its highs and lows, supporting me as I grew as an entrepreneur, and inspiring me in ways you may not even realise.

While writing this book, I had the privilege of interacting with Devika Vaidya, a Team India player with many accolades, about the journey and struggles involving Women's Cricket in India and what a young, aspiring woman cricketer or athlete should be ready for. Her insights proved to be invaluable and helped me write the chapter on women's cricket. Thank you, Devika, for your valuable insights and for sparing the time for my book.

Writing this book was always a dream, but I needed the right push and the right plan of action. A special thanks to Yash (Suyesh)

Nair and Apoorva Kulkarni, my dear friends and the founders of Devakey Digital Solutions Pvt Ltd, for believing in my knowledge and analysis of the game. Your encouragement, creativity, and unwavering support made this book possible, and I'm deeply grateful for the journey we've shared over the past year.

A special thanks to DCP Pournima Gaekwad, who always encouraged me and proactively guided me while I worked on this book. She has been a source of inspiration both in my entrepreneurial and cricketing journey and now as I begin a new chapter in my life as an author.

To all the silent supporters who have watched and appreciated my efforts from afar, I see you, and I thank you for your quiet yet meaningful encouragement.

Finally, my deepest gratitude goes to someone who will always be family, my dearest Tanmayee. You've been my anchor during times of turmoil, reminding me there's more to life than just a game. Your support and the ability to help me find joy in life's simple pleasures have been invaluable.

Thank you, Notion Press, for helping me with the publication journey and for guiding me through the entire process. Thank you for making it easy for me.

Lastly, thank you, Atharva Ekbote, for the brilliant design of the front cover of the book. I must say, he has taken my vision and words and put them into the perfect image that I could have asked for.

To everyone who has been part of this journey, thank you from the bottom of my heart.

Foreword

⸺⸺ ❧❧ ⸺⸺

Sports has proven to be a wonderful teacher. The life lessons imparted through sports continue to have a lasting impression on one's life. I've known Akash for many years now. He is a founder at BLITZ ATHLETICS, a premiere strength and conditioning facility in Pune which trains athletes for multiple sports. His thorough understanding of sports, not just the match strategy, but the entire process from the consistent physical preparation, the mental toughness, the discipline, the nutrition and the recovery that is essential for an athlete to perform at a professional level, is a result of him being a student of the sport for the past 20 years.

Akash is the no nonsense guy you want in your corner when things are going south. His passion for Cricket and his experience as a professional player enables him to highlight the unpredictable nature of professional sports. Thus, making him a perfect storyteller to an audience that wants to engage the narrator into revealing all the behind-the-scenes aspects of a professional sports career.

This book is intended for athletes aspiring to pursue sports professionally, and parents considering sports as a realistic career choice for their child. A must read; the book delves into the challenges that young athletes face once they commit to the world of professional sports.

Akash will tell you upfront that being a sportsperson is not for everyone. It takes a special kind of mindset to keep going, knowing very well that the expected outcome isn't necessarily guaranteed. Laurels and achievements do make for encouraging conversations, but it is the losses that truly reveal character. While the losses keep piling on, it is important that athletes remember that 'this' is just a game.

Unlike the yesteryears, the sports scenario today offers abundant opportunities for young athletes to pursue sports professionally. As athletes break barriers and continue to inspire an entire nation, India is on the cusp of becoming a sports behemoth. 'Unforgiving' is a step in that direction.

– Pratap Bhonsle

Preface

Before the cricketing fraternity jumps to any conclusions, let me make one thing clear upfront: this is not a biography or an autobiography. Let's get that out of the way.

I consider myself a decent cricketer who fell in love with sports, particularly cricket, at a very early age. I've also been an acute observer, not just of the game but of people and my surroundings. I started playing cricket at the age of 12, and over the years, I've had the privilege of spending time with, interacting with, and observing the who's who of the cricketing world. How and when is a story for another day because, as I said, this book isn't about me.

I've made every mistake a cricketer or an athlete can make, on and off the field, and I've experienced almost every failure imaginable. Yet, at the age of 33, I still pursue this sport with all my heart. In addition to being a cricketer, I'm also the co-founder of Blitz Athletics, one of the most successful strength and conditioning facilities in the city, specialising in training athletes from various sports and backgrounds. I mention this because, over the years, I've had the opportunity to observe countless young athletes and their parents. Their approach towards their kids' sports careers has been fascinating to witness.

In today's world, certain privileges are seen as mandatory for kids, and not only are they mandatory, but kids are also acutely aware of them, forming opinions at a very early age. These are challenging times to be a parent. While I'm not a parent myself, and this book is not meant to teach the art of parenting, there's no denying that young athletes need to be raised differently.

Consider this book a guide, a resource for parents and aspiring professional athletes on the dos and don'ts of navigating an amateur or professional sports career. It's meant for those aiming to represent their country in their chosen sport, a daunting task in the world's largest democracy, where only a small percentage manage to squeeze through for a crack at the ultimate goal. Although I write from a cricketer's perspective, the approach to most sports is fundamentally the same.

As you read this book, you may come across certain critiques of the game of cricket. Like everything in life, cricket has two sides. I haven't included these points to discourage parents or players. Quite the opposite, I believe every athlete should experience the challenges and negatives of their sport if they truly want to excel. This book is about confronting those challenges and dealing with them in a methodical, practical way. There is a method to madness, and cricket is nothing short of madness.

For me, cricket has been a teacher about life itself. It's not just a game; it's a test. No other sport on this planet will challenge you mentally, physically, emotionally, and morally over such long periods of time. None.

Now, before you decide to move forward, let me lay out a harsh truth:

"Not every child who dreams of becoming an athlete will make it as a professional, no matter how talented they are."

If you find this statement hard to accept, I encourage you to put this book down and reflect on it. In a country of 1.4 billion people, roughly 5,000 players are selected to represent their state across various age groups, and only 30 to 50 make it to the National Team. The reality is, no matter how talented your child is, they are bound to face rejection and neglect at times, often for reasons beyond their control.

That's life. That's cricket. That's sports in India. No matter what you do, always remember that success is not guaranteed.

If you're ready to face this reality and want to help your child prepare for the tough moments ahead, then turn the page. Let's get real and start preparing for the journey.

Chapter I

Introduction

---✦✦---

"Long Off, Long Off, Long Off! Suryakumar Yadav...
Suryakumar Yadav ne pakda hai apne career ka sabse
important catch!"

These words by Jatin Sapru can be heard over and over again, but I will never forget how I felt. At the point Miller swung his bat, the ball connected, and it went straight up in the air – my heart skipped a beat! Just like my fellow 140 crore cricket-crazy country.

I felt like Shahrukh from Chak De, looking at Vidya desperately during the penalty shootouts. Time stopped for those few seconds. I knew the way Miller hit the ball; it was going to be a tough boundary line catch. Needless to say, the way SKY caught the ball was nothing short of spectacular. It all comes down to the awareness that SKY had and the way he controlled his nerves and made split-second decisions, which got us the World Cup.

After 2011, our entire country gathered on the streets, in huge numbers, and in every village, town or city on 29th June 2024. India won the Men's T20 World Cup, and the nation erupted in joy. Everyone was emotional and happy, and felt like they had won it for themselves. The old and the young, the rich or the poor, it did not matter who you were; everyone danced, screamed, and celebrated the win on the streets, like never before.

That is what the game of cricket has achieved in this country.

As a kid, while playing cricket in the street, you take a diving catch, and they call you "Ae Johnty" (for Johnty Rhodes). You try to hit and miss; they'd say, "Don't try to be Sachin" (Sachin Tendulkar), and if luck was in your favour and you hit the first ball for six, they'd call you Sehwag or Viru.

Today, if you ask any kid to name five famous cricket players, they'd have their list ready. Cricket has evolved from the rare games in the '70s and 80s when the West Indies were a force to reckon with to now where there are T20s, Tests, ODIs, World Cups, T20i WCs, WTC, Champions Trophy, IPL, Big Bash League, etc.

Other than these, just in India, there are first-class games, Ranji Trophy, Duleep Trophy, Vijay Hazare Trophy, Syed Mushtaq Ali Trophy.

Just walking down the road on a busy afternoon, you see a person randomly bowling an imaginary ball. Cricket has etched itself in our minds.

But don't worry; this book is not going to be a trip down memory lane where you are hit by waves of nostalgia. This book is essentially a handbook for potential cricketers, athletes, sportspersons, and parents raising bright, young sports stars. I am writing this book to give you the bare truth about pursuing a career in sports and especially cricket.

As a spectator watching cricket, as a fan cheering your favourite team or cricketer, you have no idea about the inner workings of the game or even the mind of a player.

My aim is quite simple, I want the next generation of players to prepare their mind, body and soul for every challenge sports will throw at them. I want them to know how brutal and beautiful cricket is at the same time. I want them and their parents to understand that your son or daughter might be super talented and hardworking but he/she still might not reach the level they envision for themselves.

This handbook will prove to be as essential as your cricket kit. It will help you comprehend the layout of domestic and international tournaments and the selection committees. You will have a better grip on how to network, perform, and keep moving up the ladder. I want to ensure that you are equipped to deal with success, failure, injuries, and even making tough decisions for your career in sport.

So if you are someone who is pursuing a career in cricket or sports, or if you are someone who is considering whether or not you should be *'all in'* for cricket, or if you are a parent to a potential athlete, cricket player, or last but not least if you are a passionate fan of the game, then this book is for you.

I hope in time, as you continue reading this book, you will find more clarity regarding your choices and you will find the mental fortitude to overcome every challenge that cricket will throw at you.

Chapter II

What is Cricket in India?

------- ❖❖ -------

Ever since I had heard of cricket, I was intrigued by the game. I was probably eight years old when I saw the game on television. I saw the great Sachin Tendulkar take on the likes of Wasim Akram, Waqar Younis, Glenn McGrath, Shane Warne, and many more.

Here's the twist to this tale: my house was one of those few houses in the 1990s that still hadn't installed a television set at home. I was introduced to the game through TVs in my neighbouring homes and with friends from the society.

But once I felt the pull for the sport, nothing stopped me. I used to sit up with a radio transistor set, listen to the live commentary, and try to figure out how the match was being played. My mother used to make requests to our neighbours to let me watch an important or milestone match in their homes. My father gave me my life's biggest goal; he said we won't buy a TV set until we get selected for a match that is telecast live. For years, this was my motivation to keep working harder, and I did end up achieving this goal!

I distinctly remember the century scored by Sachin against Kenya during the 1999 World Cup. His father had passed away only a few days ago, and Sachin had returned to play because his family insisted that it was his national duty. He took to the crease and remained unbeaten with 140 runs to his name and a win for the Indian side. For me, it was unfathomable that someone who had just lost his father had the mental fortitude to come back in just a few days and perform on a stage such as the World Cup. That was the moment that got me hooked on the game.

Such is the passion poured into the game by the Indians. And the love these players command for their dedication is unbelievable. An Indian cricket fan will look up to his favourite cricketers as gods. Legends are revered in this country.

This love is clearly reflected in the economics of the game. According to a Business Today article, the average viewership of a big IPL game is around 400 million, so you can imagine the craze this game has in our country. According to trusted sources, the net worth of the Board of Control for Cricket in India or BCCI is $2.25 billion. It is the richest Cricket Board in the world.

Over the years, the business acumen of BCCI and the marvellous talent produced by India have ensured that cricket in India achieves its full monetary potential along with sportsmanship.

The Indian team and its performance are a matter of national pride for most Indians. Hence, love is closely followed by scrutiny. Every move made by an Indian player is broadcast, amplified, and receives praise or criticism from 'experts' to the general public.

People see the players with their flashy cars, flamboyant lifestyle, and the attention they get from the general public and wish, "Man, I want that too," but only a few pay attention to the hard work that they put in, the number of hours they practise to hone their skills, or even the luck factor that plays an important role in them getting a chance to be in the team that plays for their country.

In a nation where 'cricket' is not merely a sport, a player is not merely a 'cricketer'; the pressures and the pleasures are exponential. The ratio of what the game gives you and what it takes from you is never proportionate for both those who make it to the national 11 and those who don't.

Beautiful and brutal. Giving and unforgiving.

Chapter III

In-Depth Breakdown of Indian Cricket

As a spectator, you have probably closely followed the Indian National Cricket team. You must have seen how careers shape up in our playing XI. Some players go on to have long, fulfilling careers, while others may crash and burn with only a few good games to their names.

We will focus on this career journey a little later in the book.

But as of now, the question is, how do players make it to the National Team?

Our players don't drop out of the skies, nor do selectors suddenly dream about how a player might be perfect for the National Team. There is a long and arduous journey that most players have to go through to reach the top.

And that journey begins with age group cricket.

In this chapter, I am going to go into detail about the different layers of domestic cricket and how players keep progressing age-wise and skill-wise.

Age Group Cricket

So, first of all, it is important to note that while most players start out at a young age, that doesn't mean every game they play has to be competitive and lead up somewhere on the National Team ladder.

In the Indian scenario, serious competitive cricket begins at the Under-14 (U-14) level. This is where things start becoming consequential for the player.

The age group cricket in India looks like this:

- Under-14 (U-14)
- Under-16 (U-16)
- Under-19 (U-19)
- Under-23 (U-23)

Even in these categories, there are some differences in how players are viewed by teams, coaches, and selectors as a whole.

At the U-14 level, although the kids are playing more than just 'gully cricket', it is still a little laid-back and relaxed. This is a level where natural talent and kids with passion are encouraged to keep pursuing cricket further.

Now, at the U-16, U-19, and U-23 levels, the stakes are higher. If you are a player at the U-16 level, then there is a very high chance that you will be observed and evaluated for U-19 teams and tournaments. Similarly, at the U-19 level, you will be carefully assessed to see if you fit in for U-23 and even the senior state team.

The U-19 level has gained immense importance over the past few years since this level has its own set of international tournaments, including the Under-19 World Cup.

Virat Kohli, one of the greatest cricketers in the world right now, was discovered through his performance in the U-19 World Cup back in 2008. He was the winning captain of the U-19 World Cup at that time.

There was another player who shone like a star in his U-19 days–Unmukt Chand. The promising batsman was also the captain of the Indian U-19 team. Under his captaincy, India won the 2012 U-19 Cricket World Cup. He seemed to be on the same track as Virat, but something just didn't click in the big boys' club, and his career on the Indian National Team ended swiftly.

The point here is that every player is different, and their career trajectories are going to be different. So just because a youngster plays at a certain level, it doesn't necessarily mean that they are here to stay and go higher.

Next is the U-23 level. At the U-23 level, you are playing and competing mostly against players who have now chosen cricket as their career paths. It is a tough space to survive and thrive in.

Most players who perform well in U-19 and U-23 are at least seen becoming a part of First-Class cricket, if not the National XI.

***

Club & School-Level Cricket

Once a young player starts training formally in cricket, he or she will have the opportunity to participate in school-level and club-level tournaments. These tournaments are actually what can be called the 'grassroots' of Indian cricket.

These tournaments are fantastic exposure for a young cricketer, and they allow him or her to learn through experience what it feels like to play competitively. Club and school-level cricket is the stepping stone for higher levels of competition and growth in the sport.

It would be blasphemous to write about school-level cricket and not mention the famous Sachin Tendulkar-Vinod Kambli partnership.

In 1988, St. Xavier's High School (Fort) was facing Shardashram Vidyamandir for the semi-finals of the Harris Shield Cup. Sachin was two months away from his fifteenth birthday, and his team was a clear favourite for the win. Shardashram Vidyamandir won the toss and elected to bat. After losing two wickets in quick succession, Vinod Kambli (batting at no. 3) and Sachin Tendulkar (batting at no. 4) were out on the pitch. The scorecard read 60-2.

These two boys turned the game around and created history. They scored 664 runs and did not remain out throughout the innings. Vinod Kambli scored 349, and Sachin Tendulkar had 329 runs to his name. This game, the partnership, and the unbelievable batting changed the course of their lives.

So if you thought school or club-level cricket was 'just for fun', think again.

***

District Level Cricket

The districts create their own infrastructure with limited help from the state cricket associations. District level cricket is important to promote cricket and provide young talent with the chance to show their potential. There are District Cricket Associations in India that conduct trials for cricketers in their district. There is a selection committee that evaluates the players and forms a district level cricket team.

This team then goes on to participate in District level tournaments. Getting selected for a District team is a milestone for a player. This means that you have now officially transcended the phase of amateur cricket and now have some skin in the game (quite literally!).

***

State-Level Cricket

Every Indian state has an official cricket association (for example, Maharashtra Cricket Association, Uttar Pradesh Cricket Association, etc.). These associations participate in domestic cricket tournaments. They build a state-level team which undergoes rigorous training and represents the state officially in inter-state and zonal tournaments.

The selectors of these associations are scouting for talent that can be groomed for First-Class cricket.

Cricketers who make it to the state team are serious and focused players. The stakes are very high at this level, and the pressure is intense.

***

First-Class Cricket

First-class cricket in India is the highest level of domestic cricket played within the country. It serves as a platform for players to showcase their skills and compete at a high level, with the ultimate goal of getting selected for the National Team.

First-class cricket comprises multiple tournaments held across the nation. These tournaments are prestigious, highly anticipated, and closely followed by both selectors and the general public.

- ***Ranji Trophy:*** The Ranji Trophy is the premier First-Class cricket tournament in India. It is named after the legendary cricketer Ranjitsinhji (Ranji) and was first held in 1934-35. The tournament features teams representing various states and regions of India. It is played in a round-robin format, with teams divided into groups and playing against each other. The top-performing teams progress to the knockout stage, leading to a final match to determine the champion.

- ***Duleep Trophy:*** The Duleep Trophy is another important first-class tournament in India. It features teams representing different zones of the country. The tournament format can vary, but it usually involves a combination of league matches and knockout rounds.

- ***Irani Cup:*** The Irani Cup is an annual match played between the winner of the Ranji Trophy and a Rest of India team. Although it is just one match, it is considered a prestigious fixture and serves as a showcase for the top talents in domestic cricket. In the earlier days, it was seen as a match between titans; now, however, the IPL has overshadowed its importance.

***

College Level Cricket

College level cricket deserves a special mention although it doesn't specifically fall into any of the categories described so far. It is actually an intersection between district and state-level cricket, metaphorically speaking.

Students from junior college to postgraduate level represent their college in inter-college tournaments. These cricket teams are very serious about winning championships for their college.

David Cup, one of the oldest Indian college cricket contests, had a huge fan following. It became a pathway for selection to the Ranji Trophy and other First-Class Cricket opportunities. In the bygone era, this David Cup gave Maharashtra legendary cricket players like Ajit Wadekar. The best part of this tournament was that it was a 'play to finish' game. This meant that the game could be played for up to 7 days with spectators present every single day!

Currently, the Red Bull Campus Cricket is one of the most awaited college level tournaments among players and fans. This tournament is huge. It has city-level games, then state-level and finally national-level games. The country-wide champions also get to compete internationally through a series organised by the corporation.

***

Cricket in India is multi-layered and complex, and every player has to navigate through it. Every layer will reveal more about the game and the cricketer. To successfully keep moving onwards and upwards, the cricketer must have much more than just talent. This journey from club cricket to district level to state and first-class will test not just your cricket skills but also your mental toughness, your ability to bounce back, and the way you keep growing at every stage.

Chapter IV

Women's Cricket: A New Dimension to International Cricket

In 2023, BCCI hosted the inaugural season of the Women's Premier League (WPL), the counterpart to the IPL. This tournament heralded a new chapter for Indian women's cricket and women cricketers. The first season earned revenue of Rs 377.49 crores, making it a financial blockbuster as well.

While things seem to be improving incredibly for women's cricket in India and internationally, it took approximately two decades of behind-the-scenes work for women cricketers to finally reach this point.

As a male athlete, I can authoritatively speak about the structure, struggles, and opportunities in men's cricket or sports in general. I cannot comment in a similar fashion about women's cricket or women's sports since I have not had the same experiences or been through the same system as them.

But I believe that the topic of 'Women Athletes and Women Cricketers' is extremely relevant and must be discussed through this book. I am one of the loudest cheerleaders of women's cricket and women's sports as a whole. I want India to produce more and more capable, exceptional women athletes in every sport.

Hence, I chose to go to a sportsperson who can and will guide my readers on this topic through her experience and authority. Introducing - **Devika Vaidya**, a current ***Team India player*** from Maharashtra, who has a fantastic track record and a phenomenal career so far. Devika is a left-handed batter who bowls leg-spin, making her an all-rounder. I spoke to Devika at length about all aspects of women's cricket and sports. This chapter, although written by me, is a culmination of her thoughts, opinions, and stories.

Structure of Women's Cricket in India

Women's cricket in India was earlier under WCAI (Women's Cricket Association of India). In 2006, the BCCI acquired WCAI. Until 2006, the opportunities and growth in Indian women's cricket were very limited. After the change in management, things started looking up for women's cricket, slowly.

Currently, the structure for Indian women's cricket is as follows:

Age-group cricket:

- Under-16
- Under-19
- Under-23
- Seniors

Once you reach the senior stage, you have the opportunity to play first-class cricket, representing your state and zone. Women's cricket plays inter-zonal day games and one-day games. The zonal selection is based on your performance in state cricket.

For example, Devika was selected for the Zonal games based on her performance as a Maharashtra team player.

From the senior level onwards, opportunities to play for the Indian team, WPL, and other major tournaments are open to cricketers.

Devika's Journey in Cricket

Now that you are familiar with the structure of women's cricket let me take you on the incredible journey of Devika Vaidya.

Devika began playing cricket at the young age of 6. Like every other Indian kid, she started in the gully with friends from the neighbourhood. But her parents saw a spark in Devika and decided to nurture it.

The first challenge in Devika's journey began right there. When her parents tried to find professional coaching for her, most coaches told them that they don't train girls. She ended up being the only girl at a prestigious club. The coach asked Devika to tuck her hair into her cap to train with the boys. This might seem like a very trivial detail to you as an outsider, but it just highlights how the starting point of challenges is different for men vs. women.

Devika's parents had to make a lot of effort to find opportunities for her. They had to go out of their way to create a space for her in cricket. There were many times when Devika was asked to leave the ground because the officials were afraid that since she was a girl, she would get injured while playing. She was not even allowed to play in a match and had to resort to shadow practice. Imagine how painful it must have been for Devika's parents to watch their talented daughter kept on the sidelines only due to her gender.

Devika's story is a story of endurance, a story of a 'champion mindset', and overcoming setbacks. Neither she nor her parents gave up on her talent, and things kept changing as time passed. Devika debuted for India at the age of 16 and has not looked back since then.

When I spoke to Devika, she told me that all her life, since she started playing cricket seriously, there have been no days off. As a youngster, she used to play 3 matches a day in the summer league. She honed her skills by playing in different age groups and also did umpiring. When she didn't have practice sessions, Devika helped the groundsman to understand pitch-making and ground curation. In Devika's words, "I have always stayed in the zone." This crazy level of dedication has definitely paid off since she is now considered a valuable member of Team India.

Men's Cricket vs. Women's Cricket - A Comparative View

As a female athlete or as the parents of an aspiring women cricketer, you need to be aware of the ground realities of the sport.

- Infrastructure

   Since cricket is the most popular sport in India, grounds and nets are easily available. However, the coaching infrastructure is still catching up with gender equality.

Female cricketers still find it difficult to get access to quality coaching and good training facilities. This is especially true at the grassroots level in Tier 2 and Tier 3 cities.

Things are improving for our women cricketers, but disparity still exists in the mindset of the ecosystem.

- Opportunities

  Men's cricket has a multitude of opportunities in domestic as well as international cricket. The men's team plays more matches than the women's team in any given year. There is a well-defined pathway for scouting and nurturing talent from the school level to national teams.

  In the case of women's cricket, the opportunities, though growing, are still limited in comparison to men. But thanks to the introduction of WPL, women now have a bigger opportunity to shine and show their talent. The BCCI and ICC are also making efforts to organise more bilateral series between different countries to encourage the sport.

  Compared to men's cricket, scouting and grassroots support, though growing, remain underdeveloped. This means as a female athlete or parents of the athlete, you will have to be more proactive in looking out for opportunities.

- Pay Scale

  In 2022, BCCI announced that the men and women of Team India will be paid the same. Ushering a new era of pay parity in cricket, this decision is a welcome relief for women cricket players in India.

  But this pay parity is yet to be achieved at the domestic level. Even today, first-class women cricketers have to take up part-time jobs to make ends meet.

I am sure that in a few years from now, this situation will drastically change, and female cricketers will be as financially comfortable as men.

- Fitness and Training

  As far as cricketing skill is concerned, the training for a man and the training for a woman remains the same. The technicalities of the game are the same, so the practice of becoming highly skilful is the same.

  Similarly, as an athlete, if you are expected to perform at peak fitness levels, then your fitness training will also be the same.

  However, the workload and differences in physique have to be factored in when designing programs for male athletes versus female athletes. The intensity of the training and the range of strength training will vary, but no form or method of training will be exclusive to either gender.

  Another important point here that Devika mentioned is that Indian women cricketers were very skill-oriented until a decade ago. It is only now that the significance of good fitness has dawned upon our women players. They have begun to take fitness seriously and have to undergo fitness tests regularly to qualify for selection.

Devika's Do's and Dont's for Athletes

In my discussion with Devika, I specifically asked her to share some insights for the new generation of athletes. Her guidance is not limited to cricket. Kids pursuing any form of sport can apply her counsel and excel in their chosen sport.

DOS

- If you have a natural inclination for sports, take it seriously. (This applies to the parents, too. If you see your kid show any potential, encourage it with all your heart.)

- Fitness should be your top priority.

- Be goal-oriented. Set a goal and do everything in your power to achieve it.

- Build mental toughness; you will need it more than anything else to excel in sports.

- Be self-aware. As you grow older, you will have a better understanding of your body and how it functions. Your parents and coach will not have the same perspective on many occasions as you. It is very important for you to be self-aware and stick to your ground. For example, it might be a training day, but you can feel that your body needs rest. Take that rest. Listen to your body.

- Perform your best every time you are on the field. Because performance can beat politics and advance your career.

- Be ready to sacrifice. You will have to sacrifice a so-called 'normal life', food, socialising, and so much more on this path.

DONTS

- Don't keep jumping between different sports. You can pursue two sports simultaneously, but don't be inconsistent where you keep shifting from one to the other. Devika pursued both Taekwondo and Cricket seriously for many, many years. She never slacked off on either sport.

- Don't take selection for granted. Even if the pool of talent is small (especially in women's sports), never take your selection for granted. There might be occasions where you are dropped even when you are performing well. So, always work as if your selection is on the line.

- Don't compare your child with another. This one is specifically for the parents. Your kid is unique. Don't look at some other child and pressurise your child to work harder or perform better.

- Don't get obsessed with your child's budding sports career. Parents who are actively involved in the upbringing of their children tend to get obsessed with the kid's performance, routine, and upskilling. This obsession will harm your child's growth. So take care that you are involved but not obsessed.

Devika's Parting Words of Wisdom

Building a career in sports is a collective journey, where the entire family needs to become a strong support system for the athlete. Devika's family has sacrificed a lot to ensure that she becomes a star.

Remember that pursuing a sport might not necessarily guarantee success. Every setback as you go higher will result in mental breakdowns. Therefore, building up your mental toughness is incredibly vital. Be steadfast when battling injuries, and stay positive on the road to recovery.

Finally, if you have ever loved a sport and dedicated your life to it, but it didn't become your career, make it your hobby. It will keep you fit and keep you in touch with your craft. Let it remain a part of your life and give you joy.

Chapter V

Sports & Parenting

"The fact that you cannot stop being a parent until your last breath proves that it is the most important job in the world."

A few generations ago, if a child showed any signs of becoming a sportsperson, then parents quickly extinguished that by reminding the child about academics and the necessity of finding a stable job (hopefully a government job).

But things have changed now. Parents today are more than happy to support their kids in their pursuit of a sporting career.

In fact, if you are a parent who is reading this book to help your child achieve their full potential in cricket, then you are living proof of my statements.

***

"Start them early. Start them young."

This is probably one of the most clichéd phrases I've heard, especially as far as young sports persons are concerned. Parents of young athletes and players are specifically told by society that if the child shows even a little bit of spark, they must be asked to pursue the game in all earnestness.

But what are they supposed to do when nurturing their kid in sports? Are they supposed to be on the field with them every day or just sign the cheque for the academy fees? What exactly is their role?

I've realised that most parents swing between two extremes of either indifference or lack of interest or over-enthusiasm or over-involvement.

In this chapter, I want to reveal what a parent's role should be in the life of a young cricketer or an athlete in general.

First of all, be a very close observer of your child's natural inclinations and interests. When your kid begins to show the spark to play cricket or any sport, encourage it with all your heart.

Positive verbal and non-verbal cues will motivate the child to explore the sport even more.

Generally, most kids with a natural talent for any sport show signs by the age of 8–10. However, take this observation with a grain of salt because there are many cricketers and athletes who don't show any interest in the sport by 8–10. In fact, they become interested in the game in their teens and pursue it with grit.

If your kid is already showing keen interest in a particular sport, don't make the mistake of finalising that sport as 'the one' for your 8-year old. Your 8-year old, who is playing basketball today, might be playing hockey the next year, and the year after that, he/she might be swimming. So don't force them into one lane. Give the child a chance to explore and then choose his sport. They will let you know which sport they are having fun playing and want to get serious about it.

Okay, now that you've narrowed down where your child's interest lies, what's next?

The next step is finding the right coach for the child. As a parent, it is your responsibility to find a coach who will impart not only the right lessons about technique but also about values and sportsmanship. In the next chapter, I will elaborate more on finding the right coach.

And finally, once you find the right coach, I need you to take a step back. Yes, you read that right. Step back and let the coach take over.

I know my words might sound harsh, especially to doting parents. But I've seen first-hand what happens when the parents are over-involved in the child's coaching.

They will either:

a) Pseudo-coach the kid from the sidelines

b) Impose their dreams or hopes on the child

c) Or both

This is very dangerous. This is exactly what you need to avoid. A child's psychology is distinct from that of an adult. As adults, we perceive everything in terms of results and rewards, whereas children do activities just for fun.

So when a child begins playing cricket, or starts training formally under a coach, they are still doing it because it is fun. They derive sheer joy from being on the ground. They are not seeking any other reward from this.

But the moment a parent starts pressuring their child to 'stay focused', they begin to lose interest. They begin to view the game as another chore that needs to be done. You don't want this to happen because this will kill any spark the child might show; it will kill his ability to hone the skills and improve further.

Another thing you must take care of as a parent is not to force your analysis or observations on the child. When you give your analysis to the child, you create an unnecessary conflict in their brain, whether they listen to you or their coach. This, once again, will lead them to lose interest in the game.

I personally believe that unless and until the parent has played cricket or any sport at a professional level, they shouldn't give their opinions to the child.

Some 'proactive' parents who are constantly minutely observing how their kid is learning the game are obsessed with seeing improvement and results. When they don't see the kind of results they perceived as feasible and achievable, they blame the coach. They blame the training plan, and they immediately decide to move to a new academy. In a few months, they repeat the process once more.

This type of 'Coach Hopping' is harmful to a young player because you are not even letting them settle in with the fundamentals of the game and the skills. This constant shift of teaching methods and environment will give you ZERO results in reality.

Another point you must grasp as a parent here is that if you constantly change your kid's coach after every little thing that goes wrong– "What are you teaching your kid?"

You are teaching them that it's okay to take the easy way out when things get difficult. You are teaching them that they cannot fully trust anyone, no matter what their level of expertise is. Ultimately, you are sending out the signal that it's okay to be less resilient, it's okay to not be totally committed to something, and it's okay to be disloyal to people.

I am sure, as a parent, you never want to teach your child any of this.

Parents need to remember that, at the end of the day, cricket is a skill-based game. And it takes years for skills to be built up and improved. So don't let social media, WhatsApp forwards, and your own unrealistic expectations ruin your child's interest in the game.

Under good training and good exposure, eventually, your young athlete or cricketer will start blooming. They will start participating in tournaments that go beyond the walls of the cricket academy. At this point, you need to be careful to manage your expectations.

A lot of parents who see some serious potential in their child start exerting pressure on the child. This might happen unconsciously, but it is harmful when it happens. Some parents expect their kids to perform well in every match. They begin setting goals of how many runs he should score or how many wickets she should take. This is a situation that you must avoid completely.

Don't forget your child is not a colleague or an employee who will 'thrive under pressure'. He or she is just a child who is playing against other children. Let them have the best time on the field. Let them win or lose, let them scrape their knees, and let them have fun.

The most important thing a kid should learn through cricket or any sport is to 'Enjoy the game'. This is a mantra that I hold so dear that I believe it shouldn't just be followed by the kids but by every athlete until they hang their boots. No matter what happens, whether I perform well or not, I have to cherish my time on the field and enjoy the game.

It is your job as a parent to nurture your child's interest in the sport without overstepping your boundaries. It is your duty to provide them with a loving and supportive environment at home so that they take risks on the field. It is your responsibility to hold them close when they lose and let them know it's okay to lose, but make them understand the importance of learning from their failures.

Failure is a part and parcel of life. But more so in sports. A sportsperson's life is full of failures and setbacks. There are matches after matches where the team fails, the 'star' player doesn't perform, the other team is too dominant, your bowlers aren't able to control the flow of runs, and your batsmen aren't hitting big shots.

And then there are some matches where you finally see triumph, you see victory and vindication. But on average, you see failure more often. I can't believe I have to say this, but not every kid holding a bat is a Virat Kohli or a Sachin Tendulkar, who, by the way, have seen their own fair share of failures. It is important that parents learn to deal with their kids' failures in the field and they teach the children how to deal with them in a healthy way.

Kids learn from your actions. They follow your lead. So if you can adapt to failures and move on, they will quickly follow suit.

All you need to do as a parent is teach them to 'Enjoy the game'; everything else will follow.

***

In my mind's eye, I have categorised the different types of parents to athletes. Over the years, I have seen many, many parents with quirks and wonderful personalities, but they all fall under one of the below categories:

1. The Dictators

These parents are extremely strict with the kid – 'my way or the highway' is their motto. Once they see some serious potential, they hold the reins tighter. They will put too much pressure too quickly.

Parents in this category are always judgemental and harsh with their children. They are not appreciative of any achievement on or off the field. During my growing-up years, my father, who was a taskmaster, never appreciated my achievements. In fact, I was conditioned to believe there was nothing special about me or what I was doing. So much so that none of my appearances, accolades, and mentions in the local press were ever preserved. Today, I don't have a single cut-out from any yesteryear newspaper to show what I did or how young I was when I made it to the news! In my case, it wired me to set the highest standards for myself and take this positively; it isn't necessary that it will work with everyone. Tough love works, but not always, and not with all kids, especially today's kids.

The style of parenting in this category swings between pointing out the child's mistakes and highlighting how much privilege the child has been granted. They are quick to punish and don't mind smacking the child around, both physically and mentally, for trivial reasons. I've witnessed some parents whose verbal abuse is way worse than a physical beating. Their tone and language are so bad that they tend to be more harmful and scarring than the physical marks of an actual beating.

Generally, the manner in which these dictator parents talk to the kids is so negative that the kids will lose self-confidence. These parents are solely responsible for sowing the seeds of low self-esteem, self-doubt, and cynicism in their children.

A kid who once might have some talent and potential will lose interest and run as far away from the game as possible. They will give up the sport entirely and might never turn back.

NEVER BE THIS PARENT

2. The Hyper Ones

"Look, since you didn't perform well in this match, we don't think you should be playing cricket."

This is one of the most common statements parents in this category will make. These parents are generally individuals who get too anxious too quickly. In addition, they are unable to deal with failures in a healthy manner. Now imagine the kind of impact they will have on the child's psychology.

Insecurity and over-analysis are major personality traits in this parenting style. I have seen parents paint an entire negative career graph when they see their child fail in a club-level match. In their minds, they have visualised the kid failing at the highest levels and losing it all, just over one small, insignificant failure today. And they don't stop at visualisations; they share it with the kid too!

Parents in this category are extremely insecure. They will compare their child with every other kid out there. They will feel overwhelmed if there is another kid who is performing better than their own son or daughter. On the other hand, there is overexcitement if they see that their child is superior in talent to other children. There is a total lack of balance in their approach and their perception of their own child.

The Hyper Parents never encourage the child's interest in sports or anything else, simply because they don't want to deal with their anxiety and insecurities. They will happily remind the child of how many mistakes he is making so that the child loses interest in the sport completely.

AGAIN, DON'T BE THIS PARENT.

3. The Casual Ones

"Don't worry about performance; just have fun, beta!"

Ah! The dreamy, happy-go-lucky, carefree 'ideal' parents. Every kid I know would love to have such parents. These parents are fun-loving, gentle, and supportive.

I know what you are thinking, 'These parents seem perfect. What's your problem with them?'

But the reality is slightly different. Individually, all of these traits are positive, but when you take them to the extreme, they become negative. Let me explain.

The casual parents run around with the slogan, 'It's just a game, we love you no matter what,' in a loop all the time. And when you keep saying this, what you are actually teaching the child is, 'The sport or your performance doesn't matter'.

The kid is not mature enough to look at the positive aspect of what you are saying. They will slowly take you seriously and not show dedication or sincerity towards the sport because 'it doesn't matter! It's JUST a game'.

This style of parenting doesn't build the value system necessary to pursue sports. It doesn't teach the kid to be disciplined, to be serious and to work hard. What it actually imparts on them is that it's okay to be casual, insincere with your training and practice sessions. It's okay to skip matches if they 'don't feel like it'.

Kids who grow up with such parents don't tend to be serious or focused about anything in life. They don't set big goals or have ambitions; they will just try to 'cruise' through life at a comfortable speed. They will obviously not live up to their sporting potential because they never went 'all in'. This attitude will apply to anything else they do in life since the basic qualities of focus, dedication, and sincere effort are not hardwired in their brains.

Do you see how dangerous this might be to a young mind? Kids might never perform to their fullest potential because they have never learnt to respect their sport.

SO, DON'T BE THIS PARENT EITHER!

4. The "Chamchagiri" Ones

These parents are the absolute worst. Their entire focus is on teaching their kids how to stay in the good books of coaches, captains, or anyone influential rather than developing actual skill. The only skill they are teaching their kid at this point is

"Chamchagiri". These parents make their children borderline bootlickers, so much so that they stop emphasizing on hard work.

Instead, their kids are busy running around, wishing coaches "good morning" and "goodbye" like it's some sort of strategy for success. Yes, manners matter. Yes, being cordial is important. But if the only intention is to be seen rather than to improve, it's a complete waste of time.

What these parents don't understand is that their child will be noticed for one reason alone—consistent performance. Not because they hang around the coach like a lost puppy or try to be the captain's best friend. Building a natural rapport with teammates or mentors is different. But forcing it, faking it, or prioritizing it over performance? That's a straight-up recipe for failure.

As these kids grow up, they realize they've spent years trying to be a good chamcha, to stay in the good books instead of putting numbers in the scorebooks. Maybe they get a few extra chances here and there, but that's about it.

Real coaches and players see right through these tactics, and when it gets overdone, these kids aren't just ignored—they're labeled as (you guessed it) - CHAMCHAS . The word spreads. No one respects them. And when the real competition comes, these so-called "diplomatic" players get left behind because they lack the only thing that matters—ability.

I have written about diplomacy in the upcoming chapters which is an important part but remember diplomacy is something that you learn to understand and apply as you mature. When you try to teach your kids diplomacy at a very young age you aren't teaching them diplomacy you are teaching them desperation and desperation isn't a good thing on and off the field. Diplomacy is subtle. Kids are very naïve and immature to understand that subtlety. So don't teach them something that is going to affect their self-esteem in the long run.

If you want to genuinely thank a coach, teach your kid loyalty, sincerity, and the relentless pursuit of improvement. Teach them that no amount of hard work is ever enough and that there's always room to get better. But don't send the coach's favourite food through your kid every now and then. A good coach will never entertain such behaviour, and a bad coach will just keep asking for more food.

Don't be a Chamcha and don't teach Chamchagiri.

5. The Supportive Ones

This one is a rare breed. Why rare? Because it has found the balance between gentle and tough.

They are happy to encourage their kids' interest in sports. They are okay with the failures that come, and they are more than willing to go the extra mile for training and matches. They use the sport as a bonding tool between the kids and them.

But they are also smart enough to draw the line if the kid doesn't show sincerity. Their style of parenting teaches the child that discipline, dedication, and focus are a must. They will not let the kid compromise on the fundamental values.

They are very serious about instilling values like punctuality, teamwork, integrity, character, commitment, grit, effort, dedication, hard work, humility, respect, and loyalty. They are super hard on the kid if he isn't abiding by these values, but they aren't harsh when the child fails.

Basically, what they say is, "You will fail, and that's okay. But if you don't show up, don't commit 100% to the process, and don't give every match your best, then that's unacceptable."

Supportive parents are never too hard on their children when they fail while performing. They are not the type of parent who hides behind a bush and watches their kid's performance only to give them an earful later on about the mistakes they made that day.

Parents in this category are the ones who keep their hands on the kid's shoulders and tell the child how proud they are of him/her, regardless. When faced with a failure, they will take the child out for their favourite food post-match and then slip in their observations regarding the game.

The Supportive Parents fully understand their role in shaping the child's mind and psychology. Their parenting makes the child mentally and physically stronger. These kids are more focused and more committed to the game in the long run.

AIM TO BE THIS PARENT.

Whatever category you currently might fall into, make it your personal goal to become *THE* Supportive Parent. Be the parent who loves the child regardless of their success or failure but never lets them veer off course.

***

Building Mental Fortitude

Mental toughness or mental fortitude is the bedrock of success in life, especially in sports. So, if you are a parent whose child is pursuing sports, you must definitely make an effort to teach your child mental fortitude. In the later chapters of this book, I elaborate more on the need for mental toughness as well as how to achieve it. But for now, I want to share some insights with parents on how they can put their child on the path to being mentally tough.

When your kid comes to you seeking help with something that can be fixed by the kid if they rack their brains slightly, then don't do it for them. If the issue needs a little out-of-the-box thinking, encourage that and point them in the right direction, but don't give them the solution directly. Let them find a way.

There is no need to show your kid how much you know. It's okay to act dumb in front of them at times. Eventually, they will fall in love with the process of finding the solution, and they will find the answers.

***

FINALLY…

Take the time to instil values in your child. Instilling values is like planting a tree. When you plant the seed, build a nurturing environment and regularly water the sapling until one day it will become a tree that bears fruit.

Remember, every tree will flourish at its own time. Your job is to keep watering it relentlessly. Initially, you might not see it, but your kid will keep getting better year after year.

Don't focus on how much they have won or lost, or how many medals or trophies there are in your cabinet now. Focus on building the child's sense of right and wrong.

When the time comes, they will show you what they are truly capable of. Play the long game. The values you instil will help them perform eventually, if not immediately.

Instil values that will last a lifetime on the field and off the field, too!

***"Know when to be a friend to your kid
and when to be a parent."***

***

Before you move forward, I want to give you, the parents, a little homework to do. Do this, and you'll have a much better perspective on what your kid is actually doing.

#1 Fitness Assignment:

I need you to take up a fitness activity, any fitness activity, gym/swimming/trekking/yoga and pursue it for at least five years. This assignment will achieve two objectives:

1. Your commitment to any fitness activity will be a learning for the child. They will emulate you based on your 'actions', not 'words'. So lead by example.

2. The second objective is for you to understand how tough it is to stay consistent and physically fit all the time.

#2 Skill Assignment:

Your child has chosen a sport to pursue. It could be tennis, cricket, football, or badminton. Whatever sport your kid is pursuing, practise that sport on a basic level just to understand the challenges of the sport.

If you want your kid to be a tennis player, then go on the court and try playing a few shots and see how much combination of skill and strength it takes for a perfect forehand or backhand. Get yourself coached for a while to really understand the fundamentals and nuances of the game.

You will come to know what it feels like to listen to someone, especially if you expect your kid to listen to you. Understand your skill level before you go to teach them or advise them strategically.

#3 Reading Assignment:

Read autobiographies of sportspeople. Read to understand their childhood, their story, how their parents treated them, and how sports shaped their lives. You will understand an athlete's life better, and this will help you raise your athlete better.

Chapter VI

Observation and Independence

———— ✦ ————

"Observation is a superpower.
Sharp observation is half the job done."

In the previous chapters, we discussed the qualities that will make your kid tougher, both mentally and physically. But toughness isn't enough. What about making your kid smarter? How do you teach that?

Observation is key. For some, it comes naturally; for others, it needs to be taught. But the good news is that it can be taught. How? It's simple.

Whenever you're with your kid, explain the "why" behind the things they see in the world. It doesn't have to be complex; even the smallest insights can add to their knowledge. For example, explain why a road is banked at a certain angle on a turn or why electricians wear rubber boots. You could even point out someone struggling to lift a long, heavy object as a whole and explain how lifting one side at a time makes it easier, introducing them to the concept of levers. When kids understand these concepts and the science behind them, it sparks curiosity and sharpens their observation skills.

But how do you help your kid develop the power of observation, specifically as an athlete? By now, we assume your child is hooked on the sport, looking forward to every practice and enjoying their time on the field. Here are a few practical ways to cultivate observation as part of their athletic journey:

1. Holistic Observation: Take your kid to a random match, whether it's the sport they play or another sport entirely. Ask them to observe what everyone is doing: the players, referees, substitutes, and even the groundsmen. This will expand their ability to process and register multiple scenarios. The subconscious mind (we'll discuss this later) acts as a library of micro-information, which the brain draws upon when needed.

2. Micro-level Observation:

    a. Ask your kid to observe how other athletes practice or perform. These athletes don't need to be better than your child because every player has strengths and weaknesses. Sometimes, observing someone less skilled can teach valuable lessons that elevate your kid's game.

    b. Turn on the TV and study the greats. Ask your kid to observe how top athletes strategise, carry themselves during games, react to mistakes, celebrate points, handle wins, and recover from losses. How they speak after victories or defeats also matters. For athletes, the choice of words in such moments is critical, and the earlier they understand this, the better prepared they'll be.

3. Self-Observation: Encourage self-observation. Teach your kid to make mental notes during and after games. What did they do right? What went wrong? How did their body and mind react in key moments? What led to success, and what didn't? This habit builds self-awareness, which is critical for growth.

Let me share an example from my own life. When I was around 14 years old, I suffered from a lower back injury that lasted nearly six months. The root cause was my bowling action, but none of my coaches could provide a good enough solution. So, relying on my observations, I began studying bowlers with a front-on action instead of a side-on action. I noticed they exerted less force on their lower backs due to reduced twisting and rotation. Believing this might work for me, I gave it a try, and I haven't had a lower back injury since.

That moment wasn't just about observation; it was about independence. Imagine the confidence it gave me to find a solution for myself at 14. Observation made me independent, and independence changed the game for me.

Here's why independence is critical: someday, your child will encounter a bad coach because, let's face it, it's inevitable. When that happens, their ability to think independently and rely on their own observations can be a lifesaver.

Observation doesn't just teach independence; it also develops common sense, something that, let's be honest, many kids today lack due to over-reliance on parents, teachers, and coaches for every answer. Common sense solves problems. It bridges gaps. It prevails when nothing else does. You can't teach your kids every complexity of life or sport without teaching them how to apply their common sense.

For instance, imagine a batter who has an open stance. As an athlete, you must understand through observation, and common sense should tell you that this player is stronger when playing straight or through the on-side. This should also tell you that the batter won't be able to play through the off-side as well if such a delivery is bowled because it may take him a fraction longer than usual to get into a better position to play on the off-side.

The important thing to note is that observation isn't just visual. You can observe using all your senses. Listening is an important tool that can be used for observation. By listening, I don't mean listening to someone who is talking to you. That's a given, anyway. Listen to what a coach is telling other players, what players are talking about the game with each other, or what spectators and commentators are saying about other players. Commentators, especially retired players, analyse while commenting on the game, players, and conditions. This can be useful to you if you pay attention and listen. Spectators sometimes have unique observations themselves. Listening to the right ones might help you get that momentary result that turns the tables in your favour. With practice, you will know what to listen to as well.

Observation, independence, and common sense are the tools that will set your child apart. Start sharpening them now.

Chapter VII

The 'Right' Coach

"A good coach is a parent outside the house."

Finding the right coach isn't like couch surfing for what movie to watch tonight or shopping on a whim. It is a serious task entrusted to the parents of a child interested in sports.

Unfortunately, the kid is too young to understand the magnitude of this choice. He or she doesn't know the kind of impact the 'right' or the 'wrong' coach will have on them.

Imagine if Sachin Tendulkar's parents hadn't found Shri. Ramakant Achrekar as his coach. Shri. Ramakant Achrekar literally spotted the talent in young Sachin, groomed him to get better and better, and even took the effort of personally driving him and escorting him to matches all around Mumbai. This was the level of commitment from a coach that laid the foundation for India's cricketing superstar.

As I have mentioned in the earlier chapter, your job as a parent ends once you find the right coach for your kid. But who is the 'right' coach, and how do you identify him?

This chapter is not just for parents. If you are a youngster who has developed a passion for cricket or any other sport and wish to pursue it earnestly, then you too need a solid coach.

I am going to help you in this quest step-by-step.

Step 1: Identify the sporting academies:

In the earlier chapter, you have already identified the sport your son or daughter is interested in. Now, your homework is to look for a good sporting academy where he/she can train.

The factors that you should consider when shortlisting sporting academies are:

1. The infrastructure and accreditation of the academy
2. The collective experience they possess in the sport
3. The fees required by the academy
4. The distance from your home to the academy
5. The coaching timings or slots

Most good academies nowadays are equipped with websites and a basic social media presence. You can use these tools to get preliminary information and then visit the academy physically to look at the infrastructure and have an in-depth conversation with the coaches and staff.

I know some of these questions like, 'How far is the academy?' or 'How cheap or expensive is it?' may seem trivial at the outset. But trust me, they are important questions, too. Training for a sport is not a once-a-week or weekend-only activity; it is an activity that demands hours and effort from your child every single day. It is going to affect your budget as a parent and even your daily schedule if you are going to pick up and drop your child from the academy. So, it is better to prepare yourself from the beginning.

Step 2: Research the Coaches

Each sporting academy could have a number of different coaches within its team. There is also a possibility that the coach is the founder of the sporting academy. Either way, you will need to do some basic research about the coach.

This is what I want you to do:

- What qualifications does the coach have?

- Is he a former or current player of the sport? How far has he competed professionally in the sport?

- How many years of experience does he have in coaching?

- Does he specialise in a particular aspect of the sport (for example - bowling in cricket), and does that align with your child's talent?

- What are the different age groups he is coaching?

  This is an important one to address because not all coaches teach all age groups. Some coaches have a natural knack for handling kids but might not do well with adolescents. Every age group possesses unique challenges and requires a skilled coach who meets them at their level. Sit in and observe some training sessions that the coach is taking.

At this point, you are probably able to zero in on a couple of choices that look promising. This is where I bowl in my googly.

I am going to ask you a few questions about the coaches that you've met and liked. If you answer in the affirmative, then I am sorry, but you are going to have to look for a different coach:

1. Did the coach toot his own horn one too many times?

2. Did he try to impress you by showing you all his personal accomplishments as well as those of his students?

3. Did he make you any promises that sound unrealistic and unreasonable? (for example, ensuring your kid has a place on the District team or Club team)

4. Did he make you believe that your kid or anyone who learns from him is going to be the next superstar?

If your answer to even one of these questions is a solid YES, then please eliminate this coach from your shortlist.

A good coach will not try to impress you. They will not brag about their career and their achievements. The right coach will never make any type of false promises or set unrealistic expectations. And most importantly, they will not tell you that your kid could be the next big thing to happen to his/her sport.

The right coach has a knack for communicating with kids and young players. They know how to extract the best on the field without exerting way too much pressure on the child.

The right coach has absolutely no interest in impressing either you or your child. They generally tend to have a no-nonsense approach to the game and the training it requires.

I have seen four types of approaches to coaching:

a) Taskmaster

b) Soft and subtle

c) Laid-back and observant

d) Hardworking, Involved and Committed

- **THE TASKMASTER**

  As the name suggests, this coach is a strict one. He has a no-nonsense approach to coaching. The best example of this style is Chandrakant Pandit. He was tough, hands-on, and his players remained in line.

  The taskmaster doesn't like excuses for poor performances or for not showing up for training sessions. He runs the team with military precision. Every player training under him is a soldier preparing for war, and he prepares them to play to the best of their abilities.

- **THE SOFT AND SUBTLE**

  This type of coaching is the one where the coach takes a gentler approach with his pupils. He will let them run loose, but not out of control. They will find him approachable, and he won't be too hard on them. Gary Kirsten is a great example of this type. He has a soft personality, is never too aggressive, and yet manages to assert his authority as a coach on a star-studded team like India.

- **THE LAID-BACK COACH**

  Have you seen those coaches who just sit on the field and seem to be chilling nonchalantly? They seem too relaxed, too aloof from the proceedings. Search for some footage of Ravi Shastri during the Indian team training sessions. You will see him casually hanging out with no care in the world.

  This is the Laid-back Coach. He will appear to be casual, but in reality, he has a sharp eye and is a keen observer. He might not stand up and be hands-on, but if he makes one mistake, he will catch it. His observations are razor-sharp and deeply focused on improvement. He knows the strengths and weaknesses of each player in his camp and is a strong guide.

- ## THE INVOLVED, COMMITTED COACH

This one is a rare breed. This coach stands out because of his personal involvement in the kid. Coaches in this category literally take the young ones under their wing and groom them to the highest possible level. This coach blurs the line between personal and professional because he sees superlative potential in the child. These coaches lose sleep over someone else's kid.

Coach Ramakant Achrekar is the beacon of this category. Once he could see that Sachin had immense talent, he took it upon himself to do everything possible to help Sachin. He went as far as taking Sachin to every match across Mumbai on his scooter. He literally shaped Sachin as a player and as a person.

In my previous chapter, I was very clear on what type of parent you should aim to become and what type you should avoid. So the obvious question on your mind might be, 'What type of coach should we choose for our kid?'

In my observation, all the coaching styles work and have shown phenomenal results. A child understands that the coach only has the best intentions at heart.

It is completely up to the child and the coach to find their vibe. Their communication and relationship will grow through the training sessions.

The right coach might not have been a great or successful player, and that's completely okay!

A big misconception in the parenting circle is that a good player makes a good coach. This is far from the truth. In fact, there is no guarantee that a good player will become a good coach.

If you look at the game of tennis, you'll observe that a tonne of coaches have never played at the pro-level. Nick Bollettieri comes to mind. His unbelievable coaching skills resulted in ten players who reached the top of the International Tennis Singles ranking. He coached tennis legends like Andre Agassi, Serena Williams, Maria Sharapova, Boris Becker, and Monica Seles. He was the most widely recognised tennis coach in the world with zero pro-level experience himself.

Playing as an athlete on the field and training other athletes are two different skill sets. So don't fall for the 'glory' of being coached by a former national or international player.

Here are some qualities that make a good coach the 'right' coach for your kid:

- The coach is grounded (no show-off, no bragging)
- The coach is not in it simply for the money (of course, money is important, but it cannot be the sole factor why the person is coaching)
- The coach is passionate about the sport
- The coach has a holistic understanding of the game and what should be covered at each level of training
- The coach can communicate well with children.
- The coach is personally involved in the training and well-being of their students.

A good coach understands that they are responsible for building a strong foundation for a future player. They instil the values of discipline, punctuality, respect, hard work, ethics, team spirit, selflessness, and being level-headed in success and failure.

If you find a coach with these qualities, then just go for it!

Step 3: Step Back

It's official. Your work here is done. You have found your child the right coach, good training facilities, and an environment that will nurture his interest in the game.

Now, step back and let the coach take your kid forward, in the game and in life!

One day I decided to become a cricketer and I started doing everything it takes to become one.

– Rahul Dravid

Chapter VIII

The Transition

———— ❖ ————

"An amateur believes practice is practice.
A professional believes practice is a game they
need to win every day."

Through the course of the last four chapters, I've addressed cricket fans, young cricket players, and parents. I've been nice and polite so far. But that ends now.

Because I am no longer speaking to the outsiders. I am now directly addressing the PLAYERS, the ATHLETES, the SPORTSPERSONS. I am opening a line of communication with my folks. From this point on, the gloves come off. Are you ready?

***

SPORT IS A PRIVILEGE

The first thing you need to remember is that it's a privilege to play a sport. It is a privilege to be able to move the way you want to, to be able to compete, to be able to feel the pressure.

You are privileged that you have the luxury to be able to take care of your body, to be able to perform in front of a crowd no matter how small it is. You are lucky that you can dedicate yourself to something that is so uncertain year after year.

When you undertake this paradoxical journey of privilege and uncertainty, win or lose, you come out as a different animal.

> ***The next thing you need to understand and rote learn is that "Sports is a part of your life, but it isn't your entire life."***

Once you enter the field, give it your all. Whether it is at practice or in a game. But if you fail, do not let it bother you to an extent that you lose sleep over it and make life miserable for yourself. If you let sports take over your life, then you are tiring yourself out mentally and physically. As you do this, you're not making life easier for the people around you as well.

Note to parents: As parents, it is important for you to let the kid know that it's just a game. It is a part of your life; don't let it become your life. Your child is now at the perfect age to grasp this concept. Help them see that the world is big and there are bigger things waiting for him/her even if things don't work out in sports.

***

The Litmus Test

You've been playing a sport for the best part of your childhood and teen years. You've invested a huge chunk of your time and efforts into the sport. But how do you identify when this hobby or passion turns into something more? Something big? Something professional?

I suggest you take my litmus test. Ask yourself this:

1. Does this game still excite you? Are you still in love with the game?

2. What has your performance been like so far? (be realistic and objective in your measurements)

3. Are you ready to give this game the next 10 years (minimum) of your life by putting everything else on the backburner?

4. Are you willing to put your physical and mental well-being at stake for your chosen sport?

These are tough questions, and I don't want you to rush back with positive answers for all of them. Think carefully before you write down your answers.

The sport of your choosing is extremely demanding both physically and mentally. A sporting career means goodbye to a normal 9-5 lifestyle. You close the doors on 'work-life' balance, steady income, financial security, partying, lots of family time and a more relaxed physical activity level.

When you choose to become an athlete, you happily choose a life where you wake up at dawn and are out on the field. You are on the field and inside the gym for hours on end practising the same thing over and over again. You are constantly travelling. Your kit is your most important possession. You are obsessed with improving your skill level. You are going to be under constant pressure mentally, physically, and emotionally. You are in a ZONE that very few will understand and even fewer will experience.

Choose wisely.

***

Money Management

For non-athletes, the template is pretty simple. School > Graduation > Post Graduation > Job. By the time they are 25, most non-athletes will be starting off in jobs that pay them moderately well.

On the other hand, sportspeople have lives full of financial uncertainty. At the grassroots level in cricket, there is no money.

I've played matches where we were paid only INR 125 as allowance on rest days and INR 75 on match days. We were accommodated in small local motels with minimum amenities, and we had to make do with it. I've spent many tournaments eating simple dal chawal, nothing fancy, nothing high in nutrition, just basic sustenance.

In cricket, you start seeing some real money at the state-level. U-19 players are paid INR 20,000 per match, and U-23 players are paid INR 50,000 per match. On the days when you don't play or during the off-season, you aren't paid anything at all.

This is why money management is an important skill every athlete needs to learn. Now, there are two aspects to money management:

1. Family support
2. Alternate sources of income

Family support matters tremendously to cricketers, especially when it comes to financial support. A career in sports is not a conventional career. It does not have a defined corporate ladder to climb with regular pay hikes and appraisals. It is literally a different ballgame! Pun intended.

In my observation, athletes and artists have a similar career path, where they invest years and years in honing their craft, and then at some point (different for each person) their hard work pays off. These career trajectories are unique to these two fields. Hence, these are the two categories of people who require a lot of financial support in their early years.

If you are a parent or a family member of an athlete, please help them out monetarily because it's not their fault that they aren't able to make the same amount of money as their peers.

As far as sports is concerned, the 'big' investment is your sports kit (which lasts for years) and good training programmes. I've seen cricketers who have requested the cricket academies to allow them to pay their fees in EMIs or asked for higher discounts from their coaches. And in most cases, the academies have found a way to make it work because they can see the potential in the youngster.

I've also witnessed kids from rural areas borrow money from banks to pay for their travel and accommodation during important tournaments or selections in big cities. I've seen the passion guide them in taking these big risks.

The second aspect of money management is finding alternative sources of income. This is something that often gets overlooked by players. Understand this, while your family can take care of your basic needs (if you are fortunate enough), it still might not be enough.

You need to be creative and think out-of-the-box to build an alternative source of income. Look for sponsors, approach corporates, and keep an eye out for any athletic scholarships or subsidised training programmes. Apart from this, if you are old enough (above 18), then you can find some work-from-home jobs or complementary part-time work which will support you monetarily.

Remember one thing clearly, though: DON'T publicise your 'side hustle' among your fraternity because the people who are in a position to make life-changing decisions about your career want you to be singularly focused on your sport alone 24/7. So if this news of your job or part-time work reaches the wrong ears, it could end up tanking your selection chances. This is the sad and harsh reality of Indian cricket and Indian sports.

Another tip that I can share with you if you are a university or state-level athlete/cricket player is to look for government jobs that support your sport. The Indian Railways have their own cricket teams and hire young players. Not only cricket, the Indian Railways has an entire spectrum of sports teams, so keep an eye out for opportunities here. Other avenues include nationalised heavy industries that also have their own sports teams. You should try to join these teams through their sports quota. This type of arrangement gives players peace of mind because they are financially secure and have the freedom to pursue their sporting dreams.

*****

Fitness

If you look at cricket historically, it was a game played during the English summer season. For the rest of the year, players would be occupied otherwise. They had full-time jobs and other professions that would put bread on the table. Cricket was more of a gentleman's hobby for the summer.

As the years went by, cricket became a more professional and serious sport that was increasingly popular. The heightened popularity meant more matches, more tournaments, and more days on the field for the players.

As far as India is concerned, when we won the Cricket World Cup in 1983, cricket fever began to spread into the nation's psyche. From 1983 to 2011, India continued to grow into a cricketing nation. Winning the 2024 T20 World Cup was the fulfilment of the yearning of 1.4 billion Indians.

How is any of this related to fitness? Or am I just giving you a boring cricket history lesson?

Let me piece it together for you. From 1983 to 2011, fitness was a low priority in the Indian cricketing side. Our players spent 80% of their time on skill development and 20% on fitness. And it was okay until the last decade. But times have changed, and the sport has changed, so the approach of a cricketer also needs to change.

Earlier, the fastest pace of cricket was a One-Day International; now it's a T20 match that is played in under four hours. Previously, cricket was played only during the 'cricket season'; now cricket is played all year round. There was no IPL for the earlier generation of players; today's players have to fit into the aggressive scheduling of the IPL along with international game commitments.

Do you see where we are going with this?

If you were a player in the 1980s, you played an average of 8–10 International test matches and up to 8–10 ODI matches. Over the decades, this number has gone up, but not as a normal mathematical progression. It has gone up exponentially. The 2022-23 schedule of the national Indian team leading up to the Cricket

World Cup was 15 tests, close to 50 ODIs, almost 40 T20Is, and an average of 18–20 T20 matches in the IPL. So, we have gone from playing 20 international matches to over 100 international matches. Any stalwart or legend suggesting that skill is the only thing required and fitness needn't matter is delusional.

The 2023 schedule is pretty much like a leap year, which happens once every four years. In a regular year, our team would play a higher number of test matches and participate in more bilateral series.

It would be impossible for even the most talented player to survive this brutal schedule without peak fitness.

Selectors today are conscious of how fitness affects performance. If they see two batsmen back to back, both with the same level of skill, they are bound to choose the one with a higher fitness level. Because a fit player will get burnt out slower, there are lower chances of injury and they will be able to survive in adverse conditions more easily.

Players who are fit have longer careers. Look at Mahendra Singh Dhoni and Cristiano Ronaldo. Their fitness and exceptional reaction time allow them to play competitively well into their 40s.

Cricketers and athletes need to make fitness a top priority. I would recommend spending a minimum of 3–5 hours every day for skill development and a minimum of 2 hours every day for fitness.

Just to be clear, when I speak about fitness, it's not just physical; it's also mental fitness. An athlete's life is tough; you need to be tougher. Find ways to make yourself physically and mentally fit.

In Chapter 11 (Preparation), I will go into more detail about how to achieve peak athletic fitness. I will break it down into digestible and doable pieces of work for you.

***

Upskilling

Although I've gone to great lengths to explain the importance of fitness in cricket, one should never forget that, at the end of the day, cricket is a skill-based game. Skill is the most important arrow in your quiver.

I came across this interesting term called 'upskilling' in the context of higher skill-based education for working professionals. And I think it's pretty much relevant for cricketers too.

No matter what age and what level of cricket you might be playing, it's extremely pertinent that you keep upskilling yourself at all times. Players who don't keep honing their skills will feel lost in the professional circuit because everyone around them keeps getting better. Those who don't upskill don't survive.

In India alone, there are millions of talented players competing for that one coveted spot in the National XI. Why would you be worthy of it if you don't bring something new or an X factor to the game?

Nowadays, every move an athlete makes is captured on some camera. Every competitive tournament is streamed on YouTube or other OTT apps in real time. This means everything you thought was unique about you is exposed, and your opponents can learn and tackle it with ease the next time you are face to face. This is why upskilling and innovation are important. With every match, you need to take it up a notch.

Look at Virat Kohli; his slump was the most talked about thing in the media, amongst fans and haters. Did you see how much he had to upskill and innovate to build back his performance? Imagine if Virat Kohli has to put in so much hard work to evolve, then who are you and I to ignore upskilling?

***

Handling Pressure

When I elaborated on fitness, I made a passing mention of mental fitness. Mental fitness and handling pressure are vital elements in the overall fitness of an athlete.

As you begin playing more competitive cricket at higher levels, the pressure grows, too. There are more people scrutinising your performance, there is more at stake for the team, and there is more at stake for your career, too. Winning and losing both have serious implications for your long-term goals.

This is not easy to handle. The pressures of professional cricketers are immense. When you screw up, you are not just screwing up your performance; you are screwing up the match for the entire team.

Add to that the exceptional amount of wear and tear your body goes through every single day and more so on match days. Cricket, or any other sport, is physically demanding. There are injuries; there are strains. You have to undergo recovery and rehabilitation programmes. Cricketers often have to miss out on an entire series because of injuries. Think of the mental toll this must take on them because there's always someone else waiting to take your spot, and you will be forgotten.

The most important factor that needs to be addressed here is handling success and failure. An athlete needs to be level-headed as far as both outcomes are concerned. Winning one match or performing phenomenally once doesn't mean you are the next superstar of the game. Similarly, one failure doesn't mean that you should start doubting your abilities.

Find a balance, centre yourself and learn to stay calm in both situations. The trick is not being too positive or too negative. Stay in the present and keep your mind blank. The best way to keep your mind blank is to follow the process in every activity you do right from the warm-up till the end of the match or the practice session.

Being level-headed doesn't mean not celebrating. If you've had a great day on the field today, of course, you should celebrate, but learn to temper your excitement; don't let it affect your performance. And if you've lost or royally screwed up on the field, it's okay to feel down in the dumps. But don't wallow in it; don't throw yourself a pity party and stay there till dawn. Embrace the failure, learn from it and move on. Treat every day as a new opportunity to be a better athlete.

Players who are volatile and bad at handling pressure have a tendency to get over-confident or crumble in moments of intense pressure.

Take a step back, analyse your temperament, and work on improving it.

***

Mentors

As a player who has fallen in love with the game, there are going to be so many things about it that will leave you utterly confused and flabbergasted.

In India, while we have a huge number of fans, we have very few 'real' players. So, when you begin your transition into a professional player, you are going to have a million different questions that your friends and family will not be able to answer. Or if they do answer them, they will give you a bunch of contradictory hearsay opinions that won't help your case at all.

My advice to you is to steer clear of any non-player opinions. But then who do you turn to? A mentor. In sports, having a good mentor will go a long way. Although superficially, you might think they don't do much, let me assure you their work and contribution to a player's career is immeasurable.

A good mentor could be your coach, a senior whom you respect, or a former player who has taken an interest in your career. You could stumble across him/her unexpectedly. But when you find a good mentor, take their advice seriously.

Mentors will shape your mindset. They will teach you how to conduct yourself on and off the field. They will guide you in strategising a better game plan. They will push you to excel. A good mentor will keep you level-headed by having the right conversations with you.

I personally believe that if I had found a mentor, I would have played at a much higher level than what I do today.

In the case of many young players, their coach is their mentor. And this mentor acts as a buffer between the player and the parents. He takes the time to explain the intricacies of the game to the parents so that the child doesn't have to bear the burden of bad performances or failures alone. He can ask the parents to do or not do certain things at home to elevate the kid's performance.

A good mentor is heavily invested in you, and you can feel that connection strongly.

Keep an eye out for your mentor; they just might be the missing link between you and success.

***

Transitioning from a sports lover or a hobby player to a professional dedicated 24/7 to the sport is not easy. It is tough, it is brutal, and it will cost you everything that is considered 'normal' in life. Your life as a professional cricket player or athlete will be difficult to live and even more challenging to explain to others.

Even your closest friends won't understand why you can't miss one practice session for a party. Even your family members will not support you when you refuse to eat a laddu at a family wedding because you want to remain fit.

You will feel isolated from the rest of the world sometimes. You will feel disconnected from your family when you are in 'the zone'. Your teammates will become your core circle, and you'll be okay with that, too.

You will have to live, breathe, and dream about cricket or your sport. And yet, this game will hurt you, and you might not love every minute of it. But it will be worth it in the end.

Chapter IX

Networking, Conduct & Communication

———— ❧ ————

"Everyone on the field is your God."

We are a country of 1.3 billion people. Our national obsession is cricket. When we hosted the 2023 ICC Cricket World Cup, the entire nation was transformed into a cricket stadium. When we lost the finals to Australia, you could literally feel the heartbreak on the streets and in the homes.

When you are aspiring to be a successful cricketer in this cricket-crazy nation, the stakes are way too high. The body that officially governs Cricket for India (BCCI) is pretty much the global emperor of cricket. So, what do you need to make some headway in national or even First-Class cricket apart from talent?

The one, word answer is NETWORKING.

Networking is no longer something you may or may not want to learn; it is an essential skill set. And this skill should not be limited to cricketers only, every budding cricketer or athlete needs to know how to network and whom to network with.

But what do I mean when I keep harping on 'networking', and why am I calling it essential?

I am not a management expert or a professor, so I am not going to write a complicated definition here. Instead, I am going to lay it down in simple terms, networking is nurturing a good relationship with everyone on and off the field.

Moving to the next part, why is it important?

Well, the sports and athletic setup in India is different from that in other countries. As I have explained in my earlier chapters, it is an intertwined and complex path. Plus, everyone who is playing some level of the sport aspires to play at the highest level.

So you are surrounded by cut-throat players with the same goal as you. Mathematically, what is the probability that you will end up representing India with pure talent? Very low, right? So, how do you nudge the odds in your favour?

By NETWORKING.

Strong networking is creating a place for yourself with good relationships and good word-of-mouth publicity in the sports fraternity.

I have seen so many average players who were considered for selection only because they had a great rapport with the coaches and selectors. To you, this may sound as though I'm trying to say you can get selected by simply being a bootlicker. But that's not what I mean.

Let me put it this way: until you become an MVP or an asset to the team you aspire for, you will need to have certain qualities that will enable your growth as a player. One of those qualities is your ability to network smoothly and build professional, cordial, positive relationships with everyone around you. As a player, you must have the vision to let go of the small things that might come up to focus on the big picture. At the end of the day, cricket is a human game; it is a team game, and even your individual performance depends on the people around you (I'll reveal more about the people involved in the later sections of this chapter). You don't need to be 'best friends' with everyone, but at least be civil and amiable.

Why don't we look at two international players and their career trajectories to highlight the importance of nurturing relationships and not bootlicking, not simply being a 'yes-man' but smart, professional networking with a courteous attitude.

Kevin Pietersen from England was a fiery batsman. His performance on the pitch was phenomenal, but he had a rigid mindset. He got into conflicts with anyone, including his own team members. He never learnt to control or tone down his in-your-face attitude. It got so bad after a point that he was dropped from the National Team despite his records.

Virat Kohli was criticised for his 'in-your-face' attitude. His aggression was perceived negatively, and he was not seen as a good team player. But Virat evolved into Virat 2.0, the King Kohli. He took the criticism and turned over a new leaf. He is a much more poised and calm person now; his aggression is still intense, but it is only for the game. This has helped him immensely on his new journey.

My point is if exceptional players like Kevin Pietersen or Virat Kohli can suffer due to bad networking or bad word-of-mouth publicity, who are you and I?

Let me put in a disclaimer here, I don't think either one of them is wrong or right. Each has their fair share of consequences. It is up to you, which path you wish to take.

***

Alright, now that we have covered the basics of this chapter, let's work on the intricacies of the Indian sports network.

- **THE TEAM**

  Your team is your family in cricket or any team sport for that matter. They are the ones you play for and play with. Every win and loss is for the team. The team is above any individual player. Having good relationships within the team is crucial for your survival on the field and within the unit.

  Once on the field, understanding how to react to diverse situations and anticipate your teammates' responses, not just in terms of skills, but also physically, mentally, and emotionally, is crucial. Different individuals react differently, and comprehending each teammate's nature is key to optimising their responses during play.

  Team chemistry, bonding, and dynamics play a pivotal role here, and it falls upon management and coaches to nurture these aspects. Some teams, like England and Australia, conduct team building exercises to foster camaraderie.

  However, in our culture, while bonding is essential, its significance is sometimes overrated unless team relationships severely impact performance. Ultimately, winning depends on a team's quality players rather than organising activities solely to understand each other.

The team atmosphere correlates with performance; success enhances the team environment, while failure mars it. Understanding teammates often evolves through shared game experiences. Balancing skill development and team bonding is crucial. Spending time wisely between honing skills collectively and engaging in bonding activities is key.

In team sports, camaraderie often develops naturally as players spend extensive time together, fostering close bonds on and off the field. This camaraderie or feeling of brotherhood propels success. This can only come when you make an effort to build a good bond with your teammates.

Many successful teams didn't necessarily share a perfect bond; some even had contrasting egos. Yuvraj Singh has openly spoken about not having a close relationship with Captain M S Dhoni. Yet, their focus on winning overshadowed their personal differences.

In my personal experience, I've been part of winning teams that didn't extensively practice together, proving that victories can come without excessive team bonding activities. At the end of the day, it is all about maturity and professionalism.

My advice for you is that "your team is your core" so find a way to have good relationships or at least working relationships with everyone. Build a good network from the ground up for your future.

• THE COACHES

As a kid, you may have developed a strong bond with your coach. He knows your strengths and weaknesses, and you completely understand his approach to the sport. This is probably the most comfortable relationship in your sporting career. But this can't last forever.

As you grow older and start playing with different teams, your coaches are going to change; that's inevitable. Their approach is going to be different, your relationship with them is going to be different, and that's okay.

Just as a coach must understand their players, players must also understand their coaches. This mutual understanding is essential, across all stages. Not every coaching style may suit you, but adapting becomes necessary.

And if that's not possible for you, then you'll have to achieve a high level of self-awareness regarding your mind, body, and technique. This is a tough job, not impossible, but definitely tough. If you can't crack that, then you better learn to collaborate effectively with your coach.

Coaches differ in their approach: some prefer players to initiate requests for assistance, offering valuable insights only upon approach. Others are proactive, identifying and correcting flaws promptly. Some coaches adopt a testing approach, observing if players can self-diagnose before intervening. Even when faced with a brilliant yet unapproachable coach, finding ways to navigate the situation becomes crucial. Should you hold back to avoid conversation or confront the coach directly for your improvement?

In your career, you'll experience various coaching personalities, and each can be beneficial if you learn to adapt and build rapport. A coach who truly understands you is invaluable, a mentor you can rely on, even in challenging times, offering guidance when things go awry.

My advice to you is to take the time to get to know your coach and his coaching style. Figure out how you can optimise your skills under the guidance of the coach. It might so happen that you develop a great bond with your new coach, if not, at least build a healthy relationship that allows you to blossom into a better player.

- **THE TEAM SUPPORT STAFF**

The team doesn't just include the playing members and the coach. The team runs because of the support staff. They are the ones who keep it going like a well-oiled machine.

The Team Support Staff includes:

1. Strength & Conditioning Coach
2. Mental Performance Coach
3. Sports Physiotherapist
4. Massage Therapist
5. Video/Stats Analyst
6. Nutritionist

It is quite possible that the teams you play for may not include all these members or include more members as well. This variation happens due to two factors, one being funding and the other being the requirements of the team.

The vital information here is that your performance also depends on the Team Support Staff. These professionals play a pivotal role in your career. If you're a dedicated professional athlete, spending time with them off the field, particularly during the off-season, is crucial. Any sport assesses not just your skills but also your physical, mental, emotional, and moral capabilities over time. These experts help identify the minute flaws in all these aspects, thereby enhancing your career's longevity.

For professional athletes, having these individuals on your team during the off-season is a must.

If affordability is an issue, seeking sponsorships to cover your expenses could be a viable option. Believe me, as a professional athlete, you rely heavily on their expertise. It's an investment that yields substantial returns, sustaining you throughout your professional sporting career. Once you've assembled your support team, handling matters beyond your expertise becomes effortless, allowing you to focus solely on elevating your game and skill set.

No matter how talented and hardworking you are, eventual wear and tear is inevitable, leading to a decline in both physical and mental performance. Consider India's success in various sports, like track and field, badminton, wrestling, etc., in recent international competitions. Athletes now have dedicated teams funded by the government, yielding evident results.

Even Kobe Bryant, regarded as one of the greatest basketball players, faced a performance dip during his NBA career due to physical challenges, impacting his accuracy. Without his strength and conditioning coach, managing this issue efficiently would have been impossible.

If an average individual from the general population prioritising fitness can benefit from such professionals and facilities, why can't athletes whose livelihood depends solely on their sporting abilities?

My advice to you is that investing in these experts is a fundamental step towards ensuring a successful sporting career.

- **SELECTORS & MANAGEMENT**

This section of people is the trickiest to network with. They are in control of the team selection, promotions, organising, tournaments and so on.

The key here as a player is DIPLOMACY.

Diplomacy is a crucial aspect of an athlete's journey, often the most intricate. Knowing how to respond when faced with unfair treatment poses a challenge. I've witnessed athletes' careers abruptly ending due to their inability to navigate such situations adeptly. As humans, reacting to situations, whether positive or negative, is innate. However, players are expected to exhibit exceptional mental resilience, a test of their character.

Maintaining emotional composure stands as one of the pivotal aspects for an athlete. While spectators admire those who wear their hearts on their sleeves, this admiration wanes when such emotional displays become inconvenient. In the realm of cricket, a 'gentleman's game', unfairness can prevail. Those in power, often more ego-driven than sensible, find it easier to dismiss emotions.

Diplomacy is a skill integral to an athlete's toolkit, though some possess it naturally while others don't. If diplomacy doesn't come naturally, it's advisable to emulate it while keeping sight of the bigger picture. However, employing diplomacy shouldn't entail harming another's career or unjustly claiming someone else's rightful place. Focus solely on securing your position without infringing on others. Challenging authority indirectly by questioning someone else's selection can backfire.

Approaching selectors, seeking advice and inputs for non-selection despite performing well, can be advantageous. It showcases seriousness without being confrontational. Ambati Rayudu, a talented player, was omitted from the Indian team post the World Cup due to his inability to handle selectors appropriately.

Yet, it's vital to remember that performance precedes all. Even diplomatic approaches can be misconstrued as arrogance if not backed by consistent performance, potentially affecting selection prospects negatively.

My advice to you is, be very smart and careful when networking with selectors and management. Your words, your body language, your tone and your actions play a crucial role in building your sporting career.

- **THE UNSUNG HEROES**

Once, during practice with Maharashtra's renowned pace bowler Iqbal Siddique, a former Indian representative from 2001, he shared a saying that struck me: "Cricket ke ground pe sab tumhare bhagwan hote hai, groundsman bhi." At the time, its significance eluded me, but with the passing years, its meaning became clear.

Establishing a strong rapport and expressing gratitude to the groundsman is as crucial as it is underestimated by many players.

Here's why: Often unnoticed, a proficient groundsman maintains good relationships with selectors, coaches, and captains. A mere two-hour net session, involving perhaps 30 deliveries each of bowling and batting, may not suffice as an individual practice session to refine one's game. This is where the groundsman becomes pivotal. A simple, courteous request or sharing a cup of tea can influence him to prepare a favourable wicket, allowing for quality practice. They relay pitch preferences for specific games, and a favourable remark from them can amplify your visibility. Such positive attention can significantly impact the perception of coaches or selectors, sometimes bringing that stroke of luck players seek. This is true for Tennis as well. A mere half-hour session of hitting, or agility training on the courts, in tennis is not going to suffice. At this point, having cordial relations with the ground staff goes a long way in your personal practice.

Shifting focus to match situations, and though opinions may vary, cricket notably becomes more manageable at higher levels, particularly in batting and especially in domestic and IPL leagues. The infrastructure and conditions, ranging from ground quality to pitch standards, often favour conducive playing environments. Here, the groundsman plays a pivotal role yet again. A skilled groundsman, treating the turf as sacred, ensures top-notch grounds and pitches. Optimal conditions ease players into a state of focus, allowing them to concentrate on their individual processes more easily.

My advice to you is to be grateful to the ground staff. If you see them, interact with warmth and humility.

- **THE TEAM VS THE INDIVIDUAL**

Another tough one! What is more important your individual goals or the goals of the team? And how does this relate to networking?

Cricket, despite being a team sport, offers unique opportunities for individual brilliance. At any moment in a match, it's often one bowler facing off against a single batsman, presenting chances for individual prowess to shine. Setting personal goals like scoring a century, securing a 5-wicket haul, or making an exceptional catch is natural.

However, it's crucial to acknowledge that these milestones won't occur in every game. There are times when they might not manifest for several games, weeks, or even months. Yet, yielding to the temptation to play solely for yourself isn't a route to success.

Interestingly, I've witnessed countless instances where a player regained form by being thrust into situations where performing for the team was the only choice. This highlights the essence of a team sport – transcending individual aspirations.

You had a bad day on the field. Well, you had better move on and bowl well or bat exceptionally. You couldn't score good runs, move on and do well in fielding. You didn't take a single wicket, and you moved on and field like your life depended on it. Move on from your individual failures and move forward to succeeding as a team. Team sports don't have the time or patience for you to mope around about individual performances.

Remember, a good team can triumph irrespective of any single player's contributions. And players who tend to be selfish are spotted quite easily by everyone. Don't be selfish; keep your team's goals above your individual goals. Prioritise the team, and the team will take care of you. You will automatically achieve your goals when you play for the team.

In the ICC Men's 2023 World Cup, Australia was at one point trailing against Afghanistan. Glenn Maxwell was struggling at one end after he came 3-down, and wickets fell from the other end. In walked Pat Cummins, the Australian Skipper, when Australia was brought down to 91-7. Pat Cummins held the fort and ensured that he took no unnecessary risks whatsoever while Maxwell found his mojo.

Patty Cummins stayed at the crease for the entire match from that point forward and remained not out after they won. Don't get me wrong here; I know Maxwell played a dream innings and scored a double century while taking his team beyond the finish line. But the more important innings were played by the Skipper, who anchored the innings and got a meagre 12 off 68 deliveries while ensuring his partner's momentum was not broken and kept rotating the strike. Not once throughout the innings did he show the intention to go after glory. He truly demonstrated how playing for the team is of utmost importance.

My advice to you here is Team > Individual. Do that, and you will automatically be seen as a valuable member of the unit. You will find it easier to build bonds within the team. If you become selfish, you will soon be a pariah within your team.

***

Conduct & Professionalism

This is a vital aspect that you shouldn't just learn but master. Once you start getting paid to play, you are a professional athlete, and there is a certain expectation from you as a professional, both on the field and off the field. You need to earn people's respect for you to be taken seriously.

Unfortunately, there are way too many talented people who have never understood what being a professional means. As a result, they were never taken seriously as athletes and people.

Let me get to the point, straight away. A professional is someone who, first and foremost, shows up on time. He shows up on time for practice, for the game, for team meetings, and any other professional commitment.

Secondly, professionals will utilise their time to the fullest. Every minute spent on the ground and off the ground is only to upgrade their skills. A professional follows their routine ruthlessly and to the hilt.

Next is showing respect. A professional athlete respects everyone around him. His respect doesn't depend on the title or the net worth of the individual.

Professional athletes are extremely focused on their craft. They put their head down and put in the hard yards with laser-like focus. Also, a professional athlete is not self-obsessed. They are not someone who will simply pack their bag and leave once they are done. Professionals will make sure they help their teammates. This 'help' could be with respect to anything. Because they know their success, along with their teammates' success, is the team's success. They take responsibility for the team's success as well as failure. And most importantly, they perform more often than not. A professional athlete is reliable.

This next part has a deep impact on your professional conduct and image, social media. It saddens me to write this, but social media has become a tool for athletes to showcase to the world what they are doing on and off the field and create a certain image of themselves, even at the local-level.

It is what it is, and you have to adapt to it. If this is something you have to do, then go all out and showcase yourself as a professional cricketer (*jo dikhta hai woh bikta hai*). You have to show that you are training hard, you have to show you are practising enough, you are playing enough, and you are performing well enough. Instead of making social media your Achilles' heel, turn it into your advantage.

If you are going to be seen, then you might as well 'show' what you want to show and amplify your brand image. Be shameless.

However, note that being shameless doesn't mean you post anything and everything. Be smart. As I mentioned earlier, the sporting fraternity is close-knit, and they talk. You don't want to attract unnecessary gossip or controversies.

Here's what you MUST AVOID posting on social media:

- Partying and drinking
- Injuries and illnesses
- Controversial posts that will lead you to engage in unnecessary conflicts
- Anything negative related to any other player or organisation
- Posting a picture with any controversial personality

The point here is if you are a professional athlete, the world needs to see you only as a professional athlete and nothing else. You don't need to give anyone fodder to say anything negative about you in front of you or behind you. Keep your head down and do your work. Trust me, it's very peaceful and drama-free to live like this. The more peaceful you are, the better you will perform.

***

In business, there's a famous saying that goes, "Your NETWORK is your NET WORTH."

This is especially true for athletes and cricketers. We are nothing without the people surrounding us. We can do hours of net practice, put in time at the gym, eat right, and sleep well. But if we cannot nurture good relationships, then all of the rest amounts to almost zero.

Bonus: Player Analysis

Good Conduct

Roger Federer

When it comes to conduct, no better example comes to mind than the legendary Roger Federer. He is the epitome of grace, both on and off the court, and has rarely put a foot wrong throughout his illustrious career. Federer commands universal respect, making him perhaps the only athlete admired by everyone, regardless of allegiance.

Whether in victory or defeat, his demeanour remains impeccable. Watching him play or speak, one would be hard-pressed to find any reason for criticism, even in moments of loss. That's the aura he possesses, unshakeable belief, unwavering focus, and an ability to rise above distractions. His conduct is nothing short of perfection, even to this day.

However, Federer wasn't always this composed. In his early days, he was known for his fiery temper, frequently breaking tennis rackets in moments of anger and frustration on the court. It was his mother who gave him an ultimatum: either improve his behaviour or give up tennis. Federer took that advice to heart, transforming himself into the model of composure and sportsmanship we celebrate today.

Bad Conduct

Ronaldinho

After legends like Maradona and Pelé, Ronaldinho emerged as one of the few players capable of consistently embarrassing his opponents with sheer skill. His creativity, flair, and unmatched ability to control the ball made him a magician on the pitch, captivating fans and leaving defenders helpless. At his peak, Ronaldinho redefined entertainment in football, seamlessly blending artistry with effectiveness. He was not only a joy to watch but also instrumental in securing major trophies, including the FIFA World Cup and UEFA Champions League, cementing his place among football's greatest talents.

However, despite his extraordinary abilities, Ronaldinho's career serves as a reminder that talent alone isn't enough to ensure long-term success. Off-field distractions and a lack of discipline curtailed what could have been an even greater legacy. While his natural brilliance was undeniable, his inability to consistently match his skill with focus and commitment kept him from fulfilling his true potential. Ronaldinho's story underscores the importance of balancing talent with hard work and discipline, showing that even the most gifted athletes need more than just skill to sustain success.

Chapter X

Talent

—◆◆—

"Talent is like a fancy showpiece.
It feels good to have it at first, but worthless
in the long run."

Talent

Noun

Natural aptitude or skill:

The dictionary defines the word 'talent' as a natural aptitude or skill. The general perception of 'talent' is also a natural flair for anything from sport to art to science.

However, no matter how many times I read this definition, I always find it incomplete. A more overarching and complete definition of talent would be – a natural aptitude or skill that is honed through practice, dedication and hard work.'

Talent cannot be and should not be limited only to what nature has bestowed upon you. Of course, natural ability or skill is important, but it is not the end-all 'jackpot' that it is made out to be.

Everyone forgets to factor in practice, dedication, and hard work when measuring talent, whether it is within them or others.

Through the course of this chapter, I want to spend time establishing what 'talent' really means in cricket or any other sport and how it affects a player's career and mindset.

The Perception of Talent

Sports fans, coaches, selectors and even the athletes themselves believe that 'talent in sport' is how beautifully a batsman can hit shots or how 'gracefully' a badminton player moves on the court. Either exceptional conventional ability or an unconventional approach is seen as 'natural talent'.

The Real Talent

The real talent is much more than the inborn aptitude or gift. Think of a soldier who is a born warrior, but what if he never practises shooting or hand-to-hand combat and doesn't work on his physical fitness? Will he be able to successfully accomplish missions simply based on his natural ability?

No, he won't because he won't be as sharp as he needs to be. Talent is like a pencil. You need to sharpen it regularly to write clearly. You cannot sharpen a pencil once and expect the tip to stay as it is forever.

Similarly, in sports, only having natural talent is not enough. Yes, we all know that Rohit Sharma is exceptionally talented, but is his talent higher than Virat Kohli or MS Dhoni?

I am 100% convinced that real talent is a combination of natural skill, dedication, hard work and grit.

Natural talent does give you a head start, but hard work will take you far, far ahead. If you want to make a career in sports, you cannot take 'talent' for granted. Slowly, over time, as you forget to sharpen the pencil, it will start becoming blunt. And this is India, mind you; there are a million other sharp pencils ready in the box, just waiting to replace you.

So don't let your talent create a bubble of false security or comfort around you because others with a sharp pencil will burst your bubble in no time.

I have seen a few instances where the coaches are responsible for putting talented players on a pedestal. They allow certain players to be more laid-back than others in the team. This type of behaviour can have an adverse effect on the player's thinking. They start believing that they don't need to practise much or they don't need to put in too much effort to upskill themselves. This is a very dangerous path to tread.

Look at Vinod Kambli, for example. He was a brilliant player; in fact, he had a better record than Sachin Tendulkar when they were playing together, but his attitude cost him his career. He decided that he 'didn't need to practise'; he lacked dedication and was not disciplined enough. As a consequence of this, he failed miserably in his career. Vinod Kambli was touted as one of the most talented players ever and was well on his way to playing 100 test matches for India, but he ended up playing only 17.

In hindsight, if you compare Talent and Hard Work = 200 test Matches, you get Sachin. Whereas Talent and No Hard Work = 17 test matches. This should put things in perspective for you. Vinod

Kambli could have been one of India's biggest players, but now, he is reduced to a footnote in Sachin's career.

This is why the attitude of 'talent can triumph over everything' is dangerous, and not even coaches should endorse or support it.

While I am saying all of this, it is quite normal for you to wonder whether or not 'natural talent' really matters in cricket.

The answer is, of course, YES!

Natural talent, ability, inclination, and skill are extremely important in cricket. Even more so today than ever before. The game has changed drastically since its inception, and now there are not one or two but three different formats. To be able to perform, to adapt, and to grow in all three formats, one needs to have natural talent. There is no substitute for it.

The thing about talent is that it cannot be acquired externally. It's either there or not there. It can be upskilled, it can evolve with time, but it cannot be created. To explain this simply, there are some people who have 'Sur' in their vocal cords, even if nobody teaches them Sa Re Ga Ma, and there are some people who only depend on autotune to survive!

Unfortunately, in sports, there is no autotune. Everything unfolds in front of a live audience in an open stadium, with cameras capturing even the minutest of details.

The first step I need you to take is to identify whether or not you have natural talent in the game. Let me ask you a few questions that might help you in evaluating your talent:

- In basketball, do you possess the ability to take or grab rebounds consistently?

- In tennis, do you have the ability to serve at high speeds consistently and also return a high-speed serve successfully?

- In football or hockey, do you have the ability to be in the right position at the right time, to create scoring opportunities for your team?

- Can you read the slower deliveries coming out of the hand of the bowler?

- Can you score at the required rate of 10 runs per over every game?

- Can you finish a test match when your team needs 70 runs in 70 balls with only 3 wickets in hand?

- Do you have the ability to bat for 2 days straight to save a test match? (This is especially vital because in today's cricket, it is considered that playing big shots is the only way to score runs)

These questions are not exhaustive or complete. These are just a few pointers that will help you with your self-assessment.

You need to understand something very clearly, if you want to play any sport as a professional, you have to be able to do this successfully day in and day out, then you need talent. But talent is not about how good your cover drive looks or how good your forehand looks or how good you look while running on the field. This is only a small part that will maybe help you get noticed, but the rest has to be achieved through practice, dedication and hard work.

***

Next up, I am going to lay out the types of talent and the broad categories of mindset possessed by players.

Category I

In the first category, we have players of high calibre simply based on their innate talent. Now, these players are the ones whose natural abilities give them a one-up over all the other players in the second category. They instinctively understand the game better and have some techniques of bowling or batting that have come naturally to them. So obviously, they have a higher advantage.

There are two mindsets in this category:

- ***The Progressive***

  The athletes who fall into this category are superstars. They need very little coaching at the pro-level. They have a deep understanding of the game and their own style of playing. The progressive players work hard and are extremely passionate about the game.

  They need to be coached only when there are major flaws in their technique that are causing them to underperform or fail during the matches repeatedly.

- ***The Regressive***

  The regressive ones are supremely talented to begin with but also the worst ones of the lot. They start off with an edge because their talent makes them feel invincible. But the regressive ones are notorious for taking it for granted.

  They are into the game for all the wrong reasons, money and fame. They don't play because they are passionate about the game, or if they are passionate, they lose this passion once they start to fail.

  What typically happens with the regressive lot is that they stop working hard, lose focus, and rely solely on their natural talent.

They don't put in the effort to hone their skills or mature their game at all.

Such players start off with a bang, but eventually, they begin to fade. Their incompetencies begin to show; what starts out as cracks slowly become fault lines that rupture with every game.

The regressive ones waste their potential and cannot be coached at all.

Category II

In the second category, I put players who rank lower on the natural talent chart. If players in the first category are highly talented, then the players in the second category are only half as talented compared to the players in the first category.

Athletes in this category are at a disadvantage at the beginning compared to those in the first category. These players might not come across as 'impressive' or 'stellar performers' early on, but they are special.

I am not going to create subtypes in this category because my logic is simple. If you are already in the second category and you have a regressive mindset, then you have no chance of succeeding in this game anyway. So stop wasting your time and move on in life.

This may sound harsh, but that's how the game works. I am just bursting your bubble before someone else does.

So, the only players in the second category are the Learners.

- ***The Learners***

  The Learners are a special breed in cricket or any other sport. What they lack in talent, they make up for in determination and hard work. These are the players who you'll find early at the nets, working out in the gym, consistently taking feedback and learning.

Learners are highly trainable and loved by coaches. They are super motivated and play for the team. They are mentally tough and are already well aware of how much natural talent they have versus the amount of upskilling they've done.

The best example of a learner is former Australian captain Steve Waugh. If you compare the level of his natural talent with other international players, then he will rank lower, but if you look at his mental toughness, his ability to adapt and grow, he was unmatched.

Steve Waugh was one of the best captains Australian cricket ever saw. He did not even possess half of Sachin's talent, and yet Steve went on to score 32 test hundreds. In a legendary Ashes test match at the Oval, Steve had two calf tears. He was advised to rest for three to six months, but he disregarded this and walked out to bat. He was not even given a runner in the match, but he scored a century anyway. There is no better example of how mental toughness triumphs over so-called natural talent.

As you are reading this, I want you to add a point to your to-do list, Read Steve Waugh's autobiography 'Out of My Comfort Zone'. (There will be more book/interview recommendations throughout our book.)

***

The Australian Cricket Board has a very unique way of selecting players for the National Team. In fact, it is the polar opposite of the BCCI.

When the Australian selectors look at a potential player, they don't just look at the current performance stats or how in-form the player is at present. They go back to all the times this cricketer has failed.

Yes, they look at all the past failures of the player. Because the selectors want to know what this cricketer did to rise above these failures and then the next one and another one. They want to know what keeps him or her going. How they deal with failure and improve from there.

In short, the Australians are not hunting for 'the next big talent'; they are looking for a player with a strong character. A cricketer who is mature enough to understand how tough the game is and persevere like it's no one's business.

This is why you will rarely find a 19 or 20-year-old in the Australian National Team. As far as Australians are concerned, character, determination, and mental toughness are more important than mere talent.

Hence, although they don't have the most talented players in the world, Australia is a team that wins in every format and every championship. India, on the other hand, has immense talent, but it doesn't translate to the same number of wins in World Cups.

To become a champion, talented players need to be ready to lose a piece of themselves. They should be ready to lose their identity as a talented player to be known as a champion. And a lot of talented athletes aren't ready to do that.

They are so used to feeling good about themselves being known as talented that they start liking the prefix 'talented' more than 'champion' because they fear failure.

All talented athletes who became world champions were never called talented by the end of their career; they were called unbeatable, they were called legends, they were called champions.

Do you still believe that 'Talent Is Everything'?

One of my all-time favourite singers, Adele, once said,

"Talent can't dictate how you move, talent can't decide how you treat people, it does not have a moral compass. Talent cannot read a room. You can be the most talented person in the world and only make bad decisions, and to be honest, talent is like it's random; you might have it, but what does it really mean? But character is observed; it is witnessed. Character is taught and it is passed down, and character inspires people around you. Character is your armour."

The moral of the story is that talent kneels in front of hard work, discipline, and grit. Be talented. But be more hardworking, be more disciplined, and be more than what you are.

Sport gives back only to those who work on their talent every single day. For the rest who don't want to put in the hard work, sports will give you nothing because it owes you nothing.

Bonus: Player Analysis

Lakshya Sen

Lakshya Sen, India's latest badminton sensation, who represented India at the 2024 Olympics, is an extremely talented player. When we watched him play, there was no doubt that we were witnessing a supremely talented badminton player after a long time. No badminton player in his first Olympics has given us the hope of a medal the way he did.

His on-court awareness and the speed he showcased were breathtaking. Of course, it was disappointing that he couldn't achieve a podium finish, and he also got a lot of flak for it.

As a spectator, you might think that the criticism he faced from the stalwarts of the game was unfair because we saw him battle hard, and he showed glimpses of greatness in the four games he played. He even beat the world #4 in one of the games.

Then why the criticism, and is it justified? As an athlete, I can say there is substance in the criticism. There's a difference between a great player and a good player. I'm not saying Lakshya Sen cannot be a great player.

But you have to understand as an athlete, the Olympics don't happen every year. A great player makes sure he capitalises on the smallest opening he gets in the game or the tournament. A great player makes sure that once he gets his rhythm, he will not let it go. It doesn't matter if he's playing the rookie or the champion. All the greatest players have become the GOATs by beating the greatest players before them when the world was not expecting them to.

Whether Lakshya Sen becomes world No. 1 depends on how he responds to the Olympic 2024 performance with his talent.

Chapter XI

Preparation

————— ❧ —————

"Don't prepare to celebrate glory.
Prepare for the moments that can assure you the
glory you want to celebrate."

There is no such thing as an 'overnight success story' in sport. If you have ever seen a sports star emerge with overnight success and glory after a single game, then you are a mere spectator, not a player.

What you saw in one 'stunning game' is the tip of the iceberg. The performance that made a player into a 'star' is just the first successful performance at a high level of the game. But the player has been preparing for years and years before THAT game.

In this section of the book, we are going to focus on PREPARATION.

In the Armed Forces, troops prepare for everything. They have drills, simulations, and mock missions. They are put through worst-case scenarios so many times that when they actually step into the field, they are ready for anything. You cannot win wars without preparation, it's as simple as that.

The same applies to sports. You cannot win games without preparation. You cannot be a good player, let alone a great player, without preparation. Never underestimate the power of preparation in sports, especially cricket, since cricket is a highly skill-based game.

First, let's talk about my definition of preparation. Many of you must have assumed by now that preparation equals net practice or training sessions. However, I disagree. Training sessions are just one part of preparation. In my opinion, preparation involves:

1. Skill work

2. Mental toughness

3. Physical fitness

4. Visualisation

When a player works on all four of these aspects, that's when he or she becomes unstoppable.

#1 Skill Work

Every sport requires you to prioritise your skill work. The efforts you put in to build your skills pay off big time.

However, the amount of effort you need to put into your skill work might vary from sport to sport. For example, both tennis and cricket require you to have great skills; however, the skill work for tennis is limited compared to cricket.

In tennis, players spend 3 to 4 hours every single day working on their hitting skills. They spend the rest of the day doing their agility work, strength and conditioning workouts, and even mental conditioning. Their main practice sessions involve hitting, hitting, and some more hitting.

In cricket, on the other hand, players are in the net sessions for 2–3 hours with an entire team. Their practice sessions don't just involve working on a single skill.

First of all, in a team sport, your practice time as an individual is limited. You have to work around the team schedule. So, if you are a batsman, you might get around half an hour of unbroken practice. If you are a bowler, you might get an hour of bowling in rotation with other bowlers.

Although cricket is a team sport, ultimately, if you break it down, ball-by-ball, it becomes a one-on-one game. When a bowler bowls to a batsman, it's just about the two of them, bowler vs batsman. The minds of both players work at lightning-fast speed, anticipating what the other one will do. So, ultimately, it becomes an individual vs. individual sport where your skills matter a whole lot more!

This means you have to take the time out for extra practice. Try to create opportunities where you practice with players who are better than you. You have to make the effort to go back on the field and work extra on your skills. Only then you'll get a better grip on your abilities as a cricketer.

***

Practice Checklist

Okay, so when you start making time for your practice, what are you going to do? How are you going to optimise your skill work in your limited time?

Now, here's what differentiates amateurs and pros. Amateurs will only keep working, while the pros will work with a goal in mind.

You can start with something as simple as a daily practice checklist. Write down your practice goals on a sheet of paper before you go to the session, and you can add a tick mark once it's complete. For example,

- Cricket:

    1. Batting: Hit 200 cover drives today

    2. Bowling: bowl 30 good yorkers today

    3. Fielding: practice agility drills for fielding

- Basketball:

    1. Practice shooting 100 three-pointers a day

    2. Practice ball handling drills for an hour

- Badminton:

    1. Practice drills to get better at returning close to the net drop shots for 30 minutes

    2. Practice cross court returns for 30 minutes

This daily practice checklist will help you with two things:

1. Visualising your day (refer chapter 11 - Preparation for an in-depth understanding of visualisation)

2. Keeping you on track for the bigger picture

Let me give you some fabulous examples of people who have practised with a checklist in mind. Have you heard of Navjot Singh Sidhu and his famous sixes? He was an outstanding batsman who could hit with massive strength. He was one of India's prolific scorers, who used to hit big sixes and boundaries.

However, when Siddhu began playing for India, his strike rate was low, and he scored runs slowly. He was criticised for this in the press and among fan circles. So he began practising to hit 300 sixes in the nets every day. This goal kept him driven in the nets. The consistency that came with such focused skill work led to the big hits of his career.

***

Practice Schedule

How do you decide on your daily practice checklist? For that, you'll have to zoom out a little. There has to be a bigger plan in place that guides your checklist. This bigger preparation schedule should depend on two things:

1. What tournament or opponents are you preparing for?

2. What opponents are you expecting to face?

3. What conditions will you be playing in?

Find the answer to these questions and you'll know what you need to do. Preparation cannot be a random, haywire event. Preparation has to be goal-specific. The more specific you are in setting your goals and outlining the nuances of it, the better you will prepare.

Imagine you want to climb Mt. Everest, then will you prepare like a mountaineer or a marathon runner? There's a difference, right? If your goal is Everest, then you prepare for Everest.

Similarly, if you are preparing for a specific tournament against known opponents, then you have to train for it.

When the legend Sachin Tendulkar was preparing for Australia, he specifically decided to train for Shane Warne's deadly leg spin. Sachin invited leg spinners from all over Mumbai and asked the pitch curators to create underprepared pitches to help him prepare for the imminent battle between Warne and him. Every day, Sachin would show up in the nets and play hundreds of balls bowled by different leg spinners. At the end of it, when Sachin faced Warne in the test series, he dominated Warne to such an extent that Warne used to get nightmares about this.

There are many such exceptional preparation stories that we've heard and seen over the years. Take, for example, Kevin Pietersen. KP was going through a rough patch with his batting. He was repeatedly getting out LBW to left-arm spinners. He sought different ideas and techniques to overcome this, but nothing seemed to work.

Finally, he wrote an email to Rahul Dravid and asked for his advice. Rahul identified the problem as a mental block. He told KP that the issue was wanting to protect the ball from hitting the pads, which is why, subconsciously, he was getting out. So, all KP needs to do is practice without wearing pads. If he does this, then KP's brain knows now there is no protection for his legs, and automatically, he will react better with his bat.

Kevin followed this advice throughout his practice sessions and finally, when the time came to go out and bat, he trusted the process, and it worked for him.

Preparation with a goal is thus super important. It gives every action you take a direction; nothing is aimless, nothing is random.

When Virat Kohli was preparing for a series against Pakistan, he spent a great deal of time preparing for Mohammed Irfan. Mohammed is the tallest cricketer to play international cricket, towering over 7'1. The left-arm fast bowler was lethal. Given his height, the ball used to come at a pace of 140–145 km/h from almost 10', making it almost impossible to attack it the way a batsman wants to. Virat Kohli understood this and spent hours in the nets asking sidearm bowlers to bowl from that height. The Indian Cricket Team practised bowling to Virat by standing on a three-foot stool to give the impression of Mohammed Irfan's bowling. This paid off during the series, where Virat dominated Mohammed's bowling.

So, the next time you sit down to make your skill work schedule, ensure that you set a goal first. You could have a couple of goals depending on your role in the team, but do not start preparation without a specific goal.

Once you have a goal in place, it will help you figure out a schedule. It will help you in narrowing down the areas of your skill work. From there on out, just put your blinders on and get to practice.

***

Captain's Playbook

If you are your team's captain, then your preparation might vary slightly from the rest of the team. Of course, you'll have to work on your skills; that's a given. But you also need to put aside some time for strategy and gameplay homework.

Did you know that Sourav Ganguly spent months in Australia before the Indian Cricket Team even landed for the series in 2004? He went to Australia in advance and began practising on different Australian grounds. He took notes of the pitch conditions and the dimensions of the ground in order to understand his field placement during the match, how the weather affected cricket, etc. Ganguly worked like a man on a reconnaissance mission. By the time the Indian players landed to begin practice, he had done his work. This 2004 series was the first time that India retained the Border-Gavaskar Trophy against Australia on Australian soil. This victory gave the Indian team a much-needed mental boost, a high that allowed them to dream bigger.

As the team captain, make time to strategise and build your team up for the challenge.

***

Get Coached

Another key aspect of your skill work preparation is analysing your play and working on your weaknesses with your coach. As players rise to a higher level, they will find it easier to assess their weaknesses with data analytics, statistics, and videos. You can sit down with your coach and understand what you are doing wrong. Both of you can then figure out a way to improve and overcome the weakness.

In case you are not playing at a very high level of the game as of now, and you don't have all the data at your fingertips, then you can always ask your teammates to take videos of you during the nets session. This will help you analyse your technique.

Work with your coach, mentor, and teammates to improve your skills.

Another important point I'd like to make here is that a Strength and Conditioning Coach, or SnC Coach as they're normally called, is an important link between an athlete and a skill coach. What do I mean by that? Let's take an example here. If the Skill Coach is doing everything he can to help improve the speed of the serve of a tennis player, but the spinal flexion and mobility of the tennis player aren't that great, then an SnC coach comes into play to help the athlete improve strength and mobility, that is going to allow the player to serve faster. Hence, it is very important for a skill coach to work hand in hand with a SnC coach to help the athlete attain optimal performance.

***

OFF-SEASON PREP

The off-season is a beautiful time for players. You get a little bit of rest and relaxation, and then you have enough time to train.

Smart athletes know that this time is invaluable. They utilise it perfectly to prepare, prepare, and become the best version of themselves.

What should you do in the off-season?

Step 1: Reflect. During the season, you must have noticed some flaws in your technique or a pattern that is forming that causes you problems with your game. Identify this issue or issues, and seek help from your teammates, coach, and mentor. Sometimes, the things we don't notice are observed by others. Don't feel shy or embarrassed to talk about your weaknesses; seek feedback to improve.

Step 2: Now that you know what the problem is, prepare an action plan to overcome it. Sit with your coaches, look at your videos (from matches or practice sessions), and understand what needs to be done. In this step, take the time to formulate a proper action plan that focuses on overcoming the weakness.

Step 3: Start doing well-rounded practice sessions, where you work on your weaknesses and upskill on other aspects of the game as well. Remember not to go in a 'one-track' mindset, where you obsessively continue to work on only one thing and one thing. As an athlete, you are going to face a plethora of different challenges, so prepare for all of them and not just one of them.

It is important that while you are working on your weaknesses, you don't stop working on your strengths. In the end, it is your strengths that are going to pave the way for your success.

Step 4: Be patient with yourself. Keep persevering, even if you are not able to see the desired results yet.

Whenever I think of 'well-rounded', 'holistic' practice sessions, I am reminded of Mr Cricket, Mike Hussey from Australia. The legendary batsman had a unique way of preparing for test matches. During some of his net sessions, he used to divide his batting practice into three sections:

1. Batting against a new ball

2. Batting against a semi-new ball

3. Batting against an old ball.

This ensured that he was prepared for a full day of Test cricket batting. He practised to confidently face any challenge in Test cricket whenever he batted. This type of thinking and preparation earned him the title of 'Mr. Cricket'.

And if you ever feel demotivated or if you feel like today you can skip practice, think of this quote by Henry Clay, ***"There will come a time when winter will ask what you were doing all summer."***

***

#2 Mental Toughness

The next part of your preparation is probably the toughest piece of the puzzle. In this section, I am going to elaborate on a few tools that will help you in 'toughening up mentally' for the sport.

First of all, why is 'mental toughness' important or even a part of a discussion about preparation? Without mental toughness, even the best players won't make it in a sporting career.

> ***Mental toughness is not some motivational quote telling athletes to 'be strong' or ' challenge yourself'; it's a habit built over time.***

In a way, building mental toughness is similar to building muscle or levelling up your skills. I know what you're wondering, 'how can building a mental ability be similar to building your physique or upskilling?'

What do you do to build your physique? You work out at the gym with a programme where you repeatedly target different muscle groups, and slowly, over time, you see the results. Similarly, for upskilling, you practise the technique again and again until you perfect it and then move on to the next one, correct?

That is exactly what you do with mental toughness; you practise it again and again and keep improving.

Now that we've established, 'mental toughness' isn't some gift that you either have or don't. Let's take a moment to understand what it truly means for an athlete.

Mental Toughness In Sports

Mental Toughness in sports is the ability to keep your mind completely blank and follow the process to the tee perfectly.

This might seem like an overly simplistic definition, but trust me when you stand on the field and feel the pressure of performance, this will be the most challenging thing to do.

Also, note when I use the word 'blank', I want you to learn to keep your mind neutral. There should be no inclination towards positive or negative. Just a neutral blank canvas.

In my opinion, one of the greatest players with the highest mental toughness was Australian legend Steve Waugh. Steve Waugh's level of talent was average, but his mental fortitude made him legendary. If you compare his talent to Sachin Tendulkar's talent, Sachin was way more gifted, and yet Steve Waugh's name also stands tall in the history of cricket. This is only due to the fact that he was mentally one of the toughest cricketers on the planet.

With Sachin, while his talent is not comparable to any player in the world, one must understand that his capacity to withstand pressure is extraordinary. He carried the burden of expectations of a billion people every time he walked out to bat, and yet he could focus on his performance nonchalantly. That is the proof of his mental toughness.

One must understand that while Sachin Tendulkar looks 'nonchalant' and his batting seems effortless even in situations of high pressure, in reality, it took him a tremendous amount of effort to reach that level. He has built his brain and body to stay focused and 'follow the process' to perfection. The mastery he has achieved over his craft and his process allows him to look 'nonchalant' to the rest of the world.

The question that now arises is, how do you achieve higher mental strength?

Let me break it down for you.

First of all, you must remember that 'mental toughness' is not something that can be achieved overnight. Building your mental toughness is a lengthy and painstaking process which requires a lot of patience. It is a matter of practice and conscious effort.

It is exactly what you need to practice every single day. This is what I need you to do to toughen up:

1. Before the match, start learning to put all distractions, pressure points or other issues aside. Focus on keeping the mind blank and living in the moment. I know 'keep your mind blank' is easier said than done. But what if there are some hacks that make it possible? The next time you are in your pre-match mode follow these steps to stay in the present:

Casually chit-chat with your teammates, keep the mood light and breezy. This will keep your mind off from going into 'what will happen during the match'.

Next, whenever you are doing any type of activity, like a warm-up, focus on your movements. This will keep your mind strongly tied to the present.

When it's time for fielding practice, keep it simple: follow the ball and watch the ball into your hands every ball. Your brain will be so occupied with this that it won't let your mind think of anything else.

If you are doing your knocking practice, then try to watch the ball and keep your shape with every ball. This will keep you laser-sharp and grounded in the present.

As you do this, you will come up with more ways that work best for you. Keep building on these pre-game habits to strengthen your mind. Learn to put your blinders on during pre-game time. This will make it easier to achieve mental toughness during the match.

2. During the match, once more consciously, keep your mind blank. This is extremely challenging and will not be achievable immediately in the first few matches. It will take time. However, I can give you some tips to make it slightly simpler for you:

    If you are batting, the only thing you should be telling yourself is to watch the ball like a man possessed.

    Bowling, this is slightly complicated, considering the length of the bowling activity in one delivery. To simplify it.

    1. First, focus on the run-up, i.e. the speed and rhythm, and keep yourself relaxed.

    2. Loading, transfer of weight, and release. This can change depending on the ball you have decided to bowl.

Fielding:

1. Visualise which shots the batsman might play towards you and then visualise the angles and speed at which the ball is going to come at you. Visualise how you are going to stop these balls coming towards you or going away from you. Once you have done this in your head, you have done half the job.

   For example, if you are fielding at a point, the batsman is going to cut the ball hard, drive the ball squarish, or tap and run for a single.

2. Then, the next step is watching the ball intently.

   Regardless of what you are doing in the field, batting, bowling, or fielding, you get time between overs. There is a high possibility that your mind will start wandering. Utilise this time to plan your strategy for the next overs or deliveries, regardless of what you have done in your previous overs or previous matches.

Keep reminding yourself that your only priority is your process; nothing else matters.

3. After the match, there are two different scenarios that are possible here: #1 is winning, and #2 is losing. In both situations, the first thing you must remember is that don't get attached to the result either way. That doesn't mean that you don't celebrate a victory or feel disheartened by a loss. Feel everything, but don't let it stay with you and affect the preparations for the next match. Another important thing I've noticed is that when you don't perform well, and the team loses, there will be many people around you who will directly or indirectly try to make you feel guilty about the loss. Be shameless. Feeling guilty will

get you nowhere. In fact, if you let this guilt stay with you, it will start consistently affecting your future performances, too. Instead, assess the present performance, make mental/physical notes for improvement and move on. Move on from success and move on from failures.

These are the basics for building mental fortitude. However, this is where things get interesting. Now that you know what to do, you will have to put yourself in a position where you are forced to do it consciously.

Imagine that you are a bowler, and currently, your team is in the 49th over of a one-day match. The opposite team needs 10 runs to win at this point. This is a pressure situation. Go up to your captain and ask for that last over; volunteer for it. Everyone already knows that this is a tough spot, but you take this chance to test your mental toughness. If you are able to defend the 10 runs, it will give you a high like no other and the confidence to take more pressure. If you are unable to defend the score, it's still okay because you put yourself in a pressured situation and performed to the best of your abilities. The most important thing is that you learnt something about yourself and the game.

When you come out of this match, ask yourself:

- Were you able to come up with a plan to defend those 10 runs?

- Were you able to stick to your plan throughout the over?

- Were you able to follow the process to execute the plan?

These challenging situations and questions will help you evaluate your own abilities and level of mental fortitude.

The more you repeatedly go through pressure situations, the more your mental toughness will improve. The caveat here is that you follow the steps I have outlined earlier. If you don't, then pressure situations will break you.

Average athletes picture a scenario and stick to it and don't have a plan B. Great athletes show emotional and mental flexibility by not getting too attached to the situation and being prepared for the worst-case scenario. The average athlete focuses on the end goal. Great athletes focus on the process no matter how small it is. Average athletes want to improve in a day. Great athletes play the long game. They chalk out a plan and focus on getting better slowly and steadily.

Great athletes show unprecedented emotional flexibility that is a crucial part of mental toughness. Emotional flexibility is the ability to navigate through the emotional rollercoaster you face when playing on the field. It is the ability to control, regulate, and master emotions so that you can continue to follow the process and deliver results.

***

Do you remember the first REAL match you played as a kid? Do you remember how nervous and anxious you felt when the match started? Do you still feel the same nervousness now? Obviously not, because having gone through the routine of match after match has made you immune. This is what putting yourself in pressured situations again and again will do to your mental toughness, too. It will slowly make you immune to the pressure, and you'll start delivering better in such situations.

In the tenth chapter, TALENT, I wrote about how the Australian Cricket Board selects cricketers for the National Team based on their character and the strength to face failures. This is a very important learning for everyone who wants to improve their mental toughness.

As a sportsperson, remember you are going to fail more than you succeed. If you can make peace with this and still love the game, then you have the right mindset for growth in this career. Success is never guaranteed in sports. Believe it or not, you are going to fail at everything you practised at some point or another. But if you have toughness imbibed in your brain, then you will pick up the pieces and fight again.

Look at Virat Kohli or Sachin Tendulkar, who came out to bat after losing their respective fathers. Can you imagine the kind of mental strength it must have taken to stay focused and follow the process of watching the ball and reacting to it in the best possible way, considering what they were going through?

Look at Anil Kumble coming out of the pavilion to bowl against the West Indies with a broken jaw. Picture the amount of mental strength necessary to put your pain aside and bowl for your country.

My favourite example, however, is not an Indian player. It is the Australian wicketkeeper-batsman, Adam Gilchrist. When Australia was touring South Africa in 2002, some British guy sent out an email to over 400,000 people stating that Adam's newborn son Harry was not his but that of Michael Slater (another Australian player). This rumour went so viral that when Gilchrist walked out to bat, he noticed a big sign that read, 'Who's your daddy, Harry? Is it Slater, Slater?' The crowd constantly shouted and reminded him of this fake news. But Adam fought through all of this and scored 204 in the test match against South Africa, lit the entire series on fire.

These are the epitomes of high mental toughness. That is your goal. The next time you find yourself under pressure, remember the words of tennis GOAT Billie Jean King, "Pressure is a privilege."

***

#3 Physical Fitness

No one, I repeat, no one can become a successful athlete without physical fitness. No matter what sport you are playing, no matter how old you are and at what level you compete, if you aren't physically fit, you won't go very far. As harsh as this sounds, it is the truth, and I am not someone who will sugarcoat it for you.

In this section, I first want to address the parents of young kids who are interested in sports. This is going to hurt, but I have to say it, Indian athletes have remained behind in sports only because parents have been reluctant to send their kids to the gym to get stronger.

Our children are kept so far from strength and conditioning workouts that they don't develop the fitness necessary to conquer the sporting world.

So if YOU are a PARENT reading this book, please do your kid a favour and get them enrolled in a good gym under a good coach.

Now the natural question is when or at what age should children start strength training? My opinion is that until the age of 12, it's okay if the child sticks to on-field training. They don't need to be inside the gym. They are growing, already super active with games and other sports, so let them be.

After the age of 12, however, if they are sincere and focused on making a mark in the sporting world, then they must begin strength and conditioning. International Olympic athletes and champions typically begin strength training between the ages of 8 and 10. By suggesting a starting age of 12, we are being quite lenient.

Parents, here's a small do's and don'ts list to make your life easier:

DOs

1. Enrol them in a gym under a good coach.

2. Keep the association with the Strength & Conditioning Coach for the long run. Maintaining a long-term relationship with a Strength & Conditioning Coach is crucial for sustained athletic development. A consistent coach can tailor training programmes to your child's evolving needs, ensuring progress and reducing the risk of injury. Over time, the coach gains a deeper understanding of your kid's strengths, weaknesses, and goals, allowing for more personalised and effective training. This continuity also fosters trust and motivation, which plays an important role in enhancing a young child's confidence and abilities.

3. Encourage your kid to explore other sports too. Other sports help the child become aware of different movement patterns, mental freedom of playing without any burden of expectations and the chance to explore what their body is capable of.

DON'Ts

1. Don't try to be their strength and conditioning coach. You're not an expert. You can't expect your child to show results based on advice from a field you know nothing about.

2. Don't ask the coach to restrict their weight training. Limiting weight training hinders your child's athletic progress. Coaches design these programmes to build strength, prevent injuries, and enhance performance. Interfering with their expertise undermines the benefits and can hold your child back in their sports journey. Trust the professionals to do their job. Step away and relax.

3. Don't keep switching coaches. Constantly changing coaches disrupts training continuity and prevents real progress. Each new coach needs time to understand your child's physiology, which delays development. Stick with one coach to ensure consistent, effective training and measurable improvement.

Stick to this, and you will witness your child becoming stronger, faster, and more efficient both on the field and off it too.

Next, we are back to the U-19 and onwards players. You are training for the profession; you are training to be the best at what you do. This means your physical fitness should be in top form.

At this stage, your training should be much more specific to your sport and the position you play in the sport.

For example, if you are a batsman in cricket, train specifically in the gym and on the field. If you are a goalkeeper in football, ensure that you train for that role.

Don't do generic workout programmes and generic training on the field. Focus on your role like Arjun focused on the bird's eye. If you can channel that level of focus in your fitness training, then no one can stop you from being the best.

But first, why is physical fitness so important?

There are many athletes I've seen in different sports who had immense talent and skills but never worked on their physical fitness. Do you know what happened to them?

They struggled to perform on the field, had a shorter career compared to someone who was fitter, and last but not least, they never lived up to their fullest potential. DO NOT BE ONE OF THEM.

Let me show you examples of how lower physical fitness manifests in cricket:

1. For Batsmen, fatigue when running between the wickets, not fast enough to take quick runs, lower strength doesn't allow you to make big shots, and not able to stay on the wicket for long periods of time.

2. For Bowlers, lack the stamina to bowl more than 2-3 overs; as the overs go on, the bowling speed dips, and they perform poorly in fielding.

3. For Fielders, slower reflexes and the inability to run fast or dive properly.

4. For Wicket Keepers, slower reflexes, fatigue from standing in the same position, unable to move laterally with efficiency, perform poorly in batting.

If you notice these signs, then you do need to work on your physical fitness. Being fit will help you perform better.

Do you remember Virat Kohli's famous interview, where he said that he could visualise how to take the catch, but his body didn't have the ability to perform it in a split-second? He felt he was too slow. But as he worked hard on his physical fitness, he was able to achieve it.

Today, he is one of the best players in the world. There are very few athletes who could compete with his fitness level.

Imagine if a GOAT like Virat Kohli works so hard on his physical fitness, who are you and I to say no to fitness?

Physical Training

Although cricket is a skill-based game, considering the number of formats and the number of matches being played today, even at the local-level, fitness has now become equally important along with skill. You will have a lot of former cricketers who played in the 80s or 90s saying fitness is fancy, and cricket is all about practising your skill more; a 30-minute run every day is enough fitness.

Wrong. Gone are the days when running long distances for hours was fitness. In today's cricket, the game has become so explosive that every other batsman hits a 100m six, and every other bowler is bowling at 140kmph. You will not survive if you are not strong enough and fast enough. How fit you are going to be will all depend on how you train and what you eat.

A good strength and conditioning programme and a good strength and conditioning coach, as mentioned earlier, are very important if you want to compete at the top level day in and day out.

What is strength and conditioning? Strength and conditioning is a fitness programme designed to help you get stronger, faster and build your endurance levels according to your physical ability and your sport/activity. In a strength and conditioning programme, the strength part, which is the foundation of every athlete, remains the same more often than not. The specificity changes according to the activity or the movement patterns of the athlete on the field.

Let's consider the different activities on a cricket field, for instance.

Bowling

A fast bowler has to sprint at almost 20 km/h for 30 yards and almost stop himself by jumping from one leg to the other, bearing a load of almost 8 times his body weight on that leg for a short period of time, and then transfer the weight forward and behind the ball to bowl a ball at a decent pace. And he has to do this for an average of 120 times in a test match and 60 times in a one-day game. Imagine the amount of strength and mobility this requires, not to mention the fatigue that sets in over and over as he has to field as well.

Batting

A batsman has to stand low in his stance, keeping his head as stable as possible, and then react to a 135 kmph delivery. In between, he has to run between the wickets to score runs and get ready to face another delivery with his heart rate close to or more than 130 bpm. He has to be able to do this repetitively to score well.

Fielding

Fielding is different for different field positions. A slip fielder needs to have quick reflexes; a point or a cover fielder should move swiftly laterally to cut a ball travelling at high speed. A fielder fielding at the boundary ropes should have a good arm to throw the ball to create a run-out chance.

Here you need to understand that the movement pattern for each activity is different and that a fast bowler cannot train only like a fast bowler but he/she will have to train for everything.

Your basic strength programme will more often than not remain the same, be it any sport/activity.

Specificity

This is where you have the chance to turn things in your favour on the field. A good strength and conditioning programme will have a lot of specific movements that replicate your activity on the field. A good S&C coach will make sure he challenges you with a lot of drills for speed and strength that are specific to your activity and that will help you move swiftly and efficiently on the field.

Let's also break down what type of fitness training should be followed all year round:

- Off-season training: During the off-season, as far as physical fitness is concerned, build your workout routine around strength training, prehab work, and rehab work if any niggles and injuries. Take the time to build a body that will be strong enough to last the entire season. Build strong habits to perform better.

- IN-Season Training: When the season commences, your only focus should be on maintaining strength and speed throughout the season. Secondly, do specific work as outlined in the earlier section to master your role.

When you work on your in-season training, there is a common mistake that many athletes make. They create an imbalance in the time spent on the ground practising their skill versus the time spent inside the gym training.

For example, if you are a fast bowler who spends more time doing workouts and less time in the nets, then your fitness will improve drastically but your body and the movements necessary for bowling are not in sync with this new level of fitness. This will negatively impact your performance.

Also, imagine the opposite of this: you are a fast bowler who spends more time bowling in the nets and less time inside the gym. Now, your body's fitness has declined, and it cannot keep up with your improved bowling abilities.

Hence, it is very important that you strike the right balance between working out and practising to maintain your condition throughout the season.

While you are doing all the things necessary to stay in great shape, how do you check whether you've achieved peak physical fitness?

Check for the following parameters, and you will get your answer:

Overall Parameters

1. Are you able to move efficiently on the field or on the court?

2. What is your performance chart showing through the season? (stats don't lie) Is your performance improving as compared to your previous season?

3. Has your recovery rate on and off the field improved throughout the season?

Role-wise Specific Parameters

For Batsmen:

1. Do you experience fatigue when running between the wickets?

2. Are you fast enough to take quick runs?

3. Do lower strength levels prevent you from hitting big shots?

4. Are you able to stay at the wicket for long periods of time?

For Bowlers:

1. Do you lack the stamina to bowl more than 2–3 overs at a stretch?

2. Does the speed of your bowling drop as the overs progress?

3. Do you perform poorly in fielding?

For Fielders:

1. Do you have slower reflexes?

2. Are you unable to run quickly or dive properly?

For Wicketkeepers:

1. Do you have slower reflexes?

2. Do you experience fatigue from standing in the same position?

3. Are you unable to move laterally efficiently?

4. Do you perform poorly in batting?

Keep asking and answering these questions, and you will know how your fitness is helping your game.

Listen to Your Body

A vital point that every athlete needs to remember is 'Listen to your body'. Don't look at some Instagram videos of star players and start following that routine.

If you've been an athlete since your childhood, by the time you turn 19–20, you have figured out what suits your body and what doesn't. Stick to what works best for you, and don't follow your peers or favourite cricketers blindly.

In fitness, there is no one-size-fits-all. Let's look at two great bowlers: England's James Anderson and India's Zaheer Khan.

James Anderson retired at the age of 41 and holds the record for 700 Test wickets, the highest by any bowler on the planet. As a fast bowler, speed and fitness were of the essence to sustain such a long and glorious career. At one point in his career, he probably had played almost 100 matches at a stretch without any major injury.

Zaheer Khan has often been named as India's second-best pace bowler, right after the legendary Kapil Dev. Zaheer's performance has helped India seal many victories. Who can forget his 5-wicket haul against England in England 2007?

This phenomenal bowler's career often got hampered because of being injury-prone. If you look at his career graph, he has faced many injuries that made him take a break from playing for India. He could have had a much bigger impact like James Anderson, had he not naturally been injury-prone.

The lesson here is to analyse your body and its fitness, do you have the natural fitness of James Anderson, or are you injury-prone like Zaheer Khan? Being injury-prone is nothing to be ashamed of. But it is necessary to accept that you are and work on it by focusing on your off-season strength training and prehab work.

Unfortunately, I have seen athletes being shamed over injuries within sporting circles. Everyone from senior coaches to selectors and even your own teammates shames other players who are injury-prone. In fact, players who are injury-prone are often written off, even if they are fit and have recovered.

I would like to reiterate here that there is absolutely no shame in being injury-prone. Not everyone understands the science behind injuries. Don't take what others say to heart. Keep your blinders on and build on your fitness.

Whatever category you fall into, work accordingly to avoid injuries and stay fit. We will delve deep into injury management and rehab in the next few chapters.

Where to Focus for the Best Results?

As a cricketer or as an athlete, when you work on your physical fitness, don't make the mistake of constantly basing all your training on 'improving your weaknesses'. Of course, working on your weaknesses and improving them is important, but it cannot be the centre of all your attention. In fact, give more time to sharpen your strengths. Keep increasing your strengths and watch the magic on the field.

Take Chris Gayle or Virender Sehwag, for example. They are both batsmen who hit big shots. The power they manage to create in their strokes drives the crowd wild. Now, it doesn't matter whether or not these players clear the yo-yo test because their strengths are different. Their brute power is their strength, not endurance.

Similarly, you, too, should analyse your strengths and capitalise on them.

Recovery-Oriented Physical Fitness

The last aspect I want to touch upon is prioritising recovery. More often than not, players don't take recovery seriously. This is a brutal mistake. They miss out on fulfilling long careers because they never dedicated themselves to proper recovery.

Recovery deserves meticulous attention and effort. Don't be restless, and try to speed up the process. Give it the time and respect it deserves. If you recover successfully, you are free to pursue the game in your natural flair. But if you do your recovery half-heartedly, then you may have to modify the way you play, always live with niggles, and never perform fully.

To summarise, make time every single day to optimise your physical fitness. Keep pushing your body out of its comfort zone; you have no idea what you're truly capable of until you play at the peak of your fitness.

***

#4 Visualisation

Finally, we have reached the point where I reveal the trump card of preparation, visualisation. This is the secret weapon that will assist you in your climb towards sports greatness.

Visualisation is an effective tool if used properly. In this section, I will show you how to harness it for your success.

First of all, let me start with a disclaimer, 'Visualisation is not magic'. You will not achieve your goals by simply visualising them; otherwise, there would be more Messi and Kobe Bryant than we could count. Visualisation will work only when coupled with all the other preparation factors, skill work, mental toughness, and physical fitness. It cannot be your only source of success.

What is Visualisation?

To put it simply, 'visualisation is the skill of doing what you do on the field, in the mind first'.

This simple change of sequence can have a powerful impact on your performance.

However, don't be under the impression that daydreaming means visualisation. Daydreaming is just an escape from reality, while visualisation is shaping a new reality. Visualisation is the method of experiencing the actual process in your head that will lead you to a positive result. There is a subtle but huge difference between the two.

Step-By-Step Breakdown of Visualisation

Let's start with the macro picture first, and then we will move towards the micro detailing of visualisation.

Macro Step #1 Visualise your long-term goal

For example, you want to play for Team India. This is the long-term goal.

Macro Step #2: Break it down into shorter, immediately achievable steps

In our example of becoming a national player, what are the possible steps:

1. Playing for your state

2. Becoming a First-Class cricket player

3. Playing in the IPL

4. Finally, being eligible to play in the National Team and being selected.

Macro Step #3 Start visualising the shorter, doable steps

You cannot visualise all the four stages mentioned above in one go. Instead, focus only on one goal, playing for your state. Work on your visualisation for step 1; the others will follow.

Macro Step #4 Stay in the present

It is very easy to be carried away in your visualisation. You may start off with the doable steps, but before you know it, you are lifting off the World Cup. Stop yourself and bring your mind back to the present and back to your current reality. Focus only on what is in front of you; do not go beyond that.

I am not saying that you shouldn't have the self-belief that you can one day win the World Cup. But there is a huge difference in believing, visualising, and daydreaming. Learn to identify that and focus on visualising.

Micro Steps of Visualisation

Here's where things get interesting. Microsteps of visualisation are the heart of this practice. This visualisation is specific, intense, and as good as living the moment.

When you step into a micro visualisation, I want you to visualise everything, feel it deeply, and live in that moment.

Let's take an example, you are an F1 driver preparing for the next race. What will your micro visualisation be?

1. You will start by visualising your car. What does it look like? What model is it? What colour is it?

2. Now, you will visualise the track, where are the turns, where are the bankings, and how long is the track?

3. Next, you will visualise starting the race by reacting lightning quick when the light goes green and driving through a tricky start. You will visualise exactly where you will accelerate, where you will brake and how you will make the tricky turns.

4. You will visualise lap after lap until the final lap, where you will win.

F1 drivers regularly use such micro visualisation to perform better. Due to such 'close-to-reality' visualisation, when they actually sit down to drive, they are so well prepared for every turn and every braking that there are no surprises as far as the track is concerned, which is why they can react in a split-second to the uncontrolled variables.

If you do your visualisation correctly, then it should feel like time travel. It should feel exhausting as if you have actually performed in the match. Visualisation, when done correctly, gives you the power to aptly react, to shape rather than being shaped by the moment.

Multi-Scenario Visualisation

You need to go from Nagpur to Mumbai for a match. It's a very important match. You booked a plane ticket. At the last minute, the flight got cancelled. What do you do?

You immediately make a Plan B and drive down from Nagpur because you cannot miss the match. What if you didn't have a car or your car broke down too?

Then, you would have to come up with Plan C, take a bus, borrow a friend's car, or book an intercity cab.

Since you are determined to get to Mumbai, you will do anything to make it happen.

In this scenario, you have some time, not much but at least some time, say 30 minutes each, to make new plans and make decisions.

But when you are on the field, you have only seconds, sometimes not even full seconds! This is where multi-scenario visualisation comes into the picture.

When practising your micro visualisation, take charge and visualise more than one scenario. Have backups to your primary plan because there is no guarantee that your primary scenario will play out as it is. There are more uncontrolled variables than the ones that you can control, so it is best to visualise a Plan B and a Plan C. This takes away the power a 'googly' might have on your plans!

Let's take an example of this. A runner has to sprint in a 100m race.

Steps of visualisation:

1. The runner will take a position on the track

2. He will react as quickly as possible to the gunshot.

3. He will accelerate and drive his body once he reaches top speed and wins.

4. However, in case the runner couldn't react quickly when the race started, what should he do?

5. Plan B- switch his focus to the acceleration phase to make up for the late reaction.

6. What if the runner reacted on time to the gunshot, but his acceleration wasn't up to the mark?

7. Plan C-take control of the drive phase as fast as possible to make up for the lost acceleration.

The runner has Plans A, B, and C in place. This type of visualisation increases the chances of winning because the runner is prepared for it all.

How can Visualisation Help?

Visualisation is the weapon wielded by the most powerful players in sports. It helps them strategise, set goals, and achieve the impossible.

It helps in hammering something important into your brain, so when the time comes to actually do it, your brain isn't scrambling for answers; it will do exactly what you taught it to do.

I am a fast bowler, and I know that there is a particular left handed batsman in the opposing team who is weak against an in-swing ball bowled from around the wicket. So, during my visualisation, I will start with the run-up and try to create a certain angle when I land in the crease, then release the ball with the right wrist position with the right action for the perfect in-swing delivery. I will visualise myself bowling this beauty again and again and again until it becomes muscle memory.

However, to ensure that there are no chances of failure, I will take my visualisation to the next level. I will practise my visualisation in the nets. I will repeatedly bowl the way I have visualised it.

On the day of the match, I will be able to bowl the in-swing perfectly.

The greats of football like Messi and Ronaldo all practise their skills in their heads first before they show them on the field.

It is up to you how you want to utilise this power for your career.

Things to Remember for Visualisation

1. Visualisation is individual-specific and goal-specific.
2. Just like any other skill, you need to practise visualisation to get better at it.
3. There is no specific time or place where you can do visualisation. You can do it anywhere, any time. Ensure that you do it with full sincerity and intensity.
4. When one visualisation is successful, move on to the next.
5. As you watch your visualisations manifest in real life, start upgrading your goals and your visualisations.
6. Remember, not every visualisation will be successful; your opponent might be using the same skill to outsmart you. However, never be disheartened; dig deeper.

7. If you find the right master to guide you in this journey, then learn from a master the art of visualisation.

8. Keep following this process for every goal relentlessly.

9. It won't just help you with performance; it will also help you during recovery or coming out of a bad patch in life.

10. Read the following to unlock your true powers:

    a. The Secret - Rhonda Byrne

    b. Power of Your Subconscious Mind - Joseph Murphy

    c. Becoming Supernatural - Joe Dispenza

***

Prepare like your life depends on it. Prepare for the best and the worst. Prepare because only preparation will lead to success.

There are no shortcuts; there are no magic tricks to make you a sporting legend. If you don't put your sweat, blood, and tears into it, you will achieve nothing, and that's a FACT. Brutal, harsh, and unfortunately for you, the TRUTH.

Bonus: Player Analysis

Unbeatable Preparation

Kobe Bryant

Kobe Bryant's meticulous preparation for games and seasons is legendary, and his autobiography, The Black Mamba, offers a masterclass for aspiring basketball players on the level of dedication required to succeed. While Kobe's aggressive style of play and immense talent are widely celebrated, what truly set him apart was his intelligence and technical mastery on the court.

Kobe ensured he left no stone unturned in his preparation. He rigorously studied tapes of his opponents, identifying patterns, tendencies, and weaknesses. He tailored his practice sessions specifically to counter the strengths of his opponents and the strategies of opposing teams. His ability to execute these plans with precision during games was a hallmark of his greatness.

One striking example from his book illustrates his unmatched attention to detail. While guarding an opponent, Kobe noticed in-game footage that the player consistently faked in a particular direction and attempted a jump shot after a specific interval of time. Kobe meticulously counted the seconds during the game to anticipate when the player would make the move. This allowed him to effectively neutralise the player's scoring attempts throughout the match.

Such an extraordinary level of preparation and observation, down to counting seconds in his head, underscores Kobe's relentless drive for perfection. It wasn't just raw talent but his unmatched work ethic, intelligence, and preparation that made him one of the greatest players to ever grace the basketball court.

Unbeatable Work Ethic

Adam Gilchrist

During my time as a net bowler for international and IPL teams in Pune, I had the privilege of observing Adam Gilchrist up close when Kings XI Punjab played a match there. On this particular day, the team's net session was delayed by half an hour because the pitch was slightly wet and not ideal for batting. While most batsmen took off their pads to wait, Gilchrist chose to make the most of the time. He took one of the coaches to the boundary line and began practising throwdowns until the nets resumed.

Once the nets began, Gilchrist batted for another 30 to 45 minutes, and when he finished, he didn't stop there. He spent an additional 30 minutes practising strokes, keeping his pads on for more than 90 minutes straight. Immediately after this, he switched to his wicket-keeping gear and trained against spinners and fast bowlers for another 30 minutes. Even after all this, he wasn't done. He jogged for 20 minutes and followed it up with 25 to 30 intense 30-yard sprints. His practice session lasted nearly three hours, and he was the last to leave the field. What amazed me even more was that Gilchrist had already retired from international cricket at the time.

Witnessing his dedication to both skill and fitness left me in awe. I had always thought I worked hard, but seeing Gilchrist's relentless commitment made me feel humbled. His work ethic, even after retirement, was a powerful lesson in what it truly means to strive for excellence.

Unbeatable Fitness

Dhanraj Pillay

Dhanraj Pillay is a name synonymous with excellence in Indian hockey. Over a remarkable 16 year career, he achieved what few athletes ever do, representing India in four Olympics, four World Cups, four Champions Trophies, and four Asian Games. This incredible feat speaks not just to his unparalleled skill on the field but also to his longevity and consistency at the highest level of the sport. His blistering speed, sharp stickwork, and uncanny ability to break through defences made him a formidable presence and one of the greatest forwards in Indian hockey history.

Pillay's versatility and leadership were instrumental in bringing Indian hockey back into the spotlight. Whether playing against the strongest global teams or leading India to victory in tournaments like the 1998 Asian Games, his ability to perform under pressure set him apart. Pillay's legacy is not just in his records but also in the inspiration he provided to countless young players aspiring to make a mark in Indian hockey. His extraordinary career remains a testament to his dedication, skill, and passion for the game.

Chapter XII

Injuries, Pre-Hab & Rehab

The discussion of an athlete's career or life in general is incomplete without the discussion of injuries. Injuries are a part and parcel of any given sport.

Rather, I would be bold enough to say, injuries are a part of any physical activity. What I mean is you can get injured doing mundane tasks like getting out of the bed wrong, or slipping over something while walking. These are routine everyday activities that might cause injury.

In the case of an athlete, our jobs are much more demanding physically and require putting a strain on the body in different ways, hence we are more prone to injuries.

As kids, we tend to fall more, but we recover quicker as well. The body of a child is truly magical, it heals faster than any adult body. This allows children to be more carefree in their approach to sports and physical activities. As we grow older however things change. Our bodies take longer to recover and we need to be more methodical on our road to recovery.

Hence, my first rule of thumb for athletes is accept that you are bound to be injured at some point of time or other. As I mentioned earlier, some athletes are more injury prone than others. Injury prone or not, it is better to accept that you may get injured. If you are mentally prepared, then recovering from injuries will not be an extremely tough task in your life.

Most athletes you and I see playing at the elite level, are playing with some kind of niggle in the body, many have just recovered from an injury, many are doing prehab to avoid a big injury. The truth is there is no athlete in the world who has been able to escape the cycle of injuries, rehabs and prehabs. So it is best to be armed to handle them better. This chapter is your toolkit for injury management.

Injuries can be of different types. They may be on-field injuries or off-field ones. They may be small, easily recoverable ones or big, career-threatening ones. Let me take a moment here and elaborate a little more on what factors can possibly contribute to injuries. If as an athlete you are aware of these, then you can be alert and proactively prevent injuries too.

#1 Excessive Unmanaged Workload -

As athletes, we are extremely passionate people who give our 150% on the field for our sport. So, if it is necessary for me to play a certain way with niggles or a little pain, I will continue to do so, even if it might result in an injury. For example, I remember how the "Tennis Elbow" became insanely famous when Sachin Tendulkar got injured in the early 2000s. Sachin as a batsman always used a heavier bat than average. However deceptive as the name "tennis elbow" may be, it was a result from the overuse of muscles and tendons in the elbow due to gripping activities. Sachin must have known for a long time that he was facing an issue but he continued with his usual workload because his sport demanded it.

These types of injuries are not totally avoidable, but can be managed if the athlete identifies it in the early stages. So keep a lookout for issues arising from "excessive unmanaged workload". Try to be more balanced in your approach when you perform in your sport.

#2 Technical or Biomechanical Faults

Athletes can be prone to injuries due to **technical** or **biomechanical faults** that place excessive strain on their bodies. These faults can arise due to improper technique, muscular imbalances, poor movement patterns, or inadequate conditioning. Here are some key biomechanical and technical faults that increase the risk of injuries:

1. Poor Posture and Alignment Issues

- **Excessive forward head posture** – Leads to neck and shoulder strain.
- **Anterior pelvic tilt** – Leads to lower back stress and hamstring tightness.

2. Muscle Imbalances and Weaknesses

- **Quad dominance over hamstrings** – Increases the risk of ACL injuries in sports like football and basketball.
- **Weak glutes** – Leads to knee valgus (knees caving inward), causing knee pain or ACL tears.
- **Asymmetry between dominant and non-dominant limbs** – Increases stress on the stronger side, leading to overuse injuries.

3. Faulty Running and Jumping Mechanics

- **Improper landing technique** – Landing with locked knees instead of flexed knees can lead to ACL tears or meniscus damage.

- **Lack of dorsiflexion in the ankle** – Reduces shock absorption and increases the risk of Achilles tendon injuries.

4. Incorrect Lifting Techniques (Strength Training)

- **Lifting with a rounded back** – Causes spinal disc injuries.

- **Poor core engagement** – Leads to instability and higher chances of back and hip injuries.

- **Hyperextension of joints (e.g., elbows or knees)** – Increases ligament strain and risk of hypermobility injuries.

5. Lack of Mobility and Flexibility

- **Tight hip flexors** – Restrict movement and cause lower back pain.

- **Limited ankle mobility** – Increases stress on knees and feet, leading to plantar fasciitis or shin splints.

- **Poor shoulder mobility** – Leads to impingements, rotator cuff tears, and instability.

6. Repetitive Faulty Movements (Overuse Injuries)

- **Excessive internal rotation of the shoulder (in throwing sports)** – Leads to rotator cuff tears and labrum injuries.

- **Improper swing mechanics in racquet sports** – Causes tennis elbow or golfer's elbow.

- **Incorrect foot placement in cutting and pivoting sports** – Increases the risk of ankle sprains and ACL injuries.

7. Foot and Gait Abnormalities

- **Flat feet (overpronation)** – Can cause shin splints, knee pain, and plantar fasciitis.

- **High arches (underpronation)** – Reduces shock absorption, increasing stress on the lower part of the heel.

- **Uneven leg length** – Leads to an imbalanced gait, resulting in hip and lower back injuries.

Addressing these biomechanical and technical faults through **proper training, strengthening, mobility work, and technique correction** (wherever necessary) can significantly reduce injury risk. Regular assessments by physiotherapists, strength coaches, and sports scientists can help athletes optimize movement patterns and stay injury-free.

#3 Plain Stupidity

These are **self-inflicted injuries that result from carelessness and lack of awareness** rather than natural game risks. Such injuries are preventable if athletes are alert, disciplined, and follow basic safety measures.

Read this section very carefully, because every injury in this category can be fully avoided. Think of me, every time you are about to act stupid, think of the lines in this book - and simply put "DON'T BE STUPID".

Now, for some examples of stupidity:

- Not wearing a safety gear

- Casual warm-ups before fast bowling spells.

- Kicking hard surfaces, or objects in frustration and anger

- Not tying shoelaces properly

- Over-celebrating

- Self-inflicted weight room injuries

- Playing a different sport just for fun - playing a sport that doesn't align with your chosen sport's movement pattern is stupidity.

As athletes it is our job to push the limits, but **some injuries are just avoidable if they are careful, aware, and disciplined**. Many careers have been affected by careless moments that could have been **prevented with better awareness and decision-making**.

#4 Plain Bad Luck

These injuries are completely unpredictable and cannot be factored in. I don't have any logic or answers to the "plain bad luck" injuries except that I pray and wish you don't have to face them. The classic example that defies all logic is Indian wicket keeper and batsman Rishabh Pant. The horrific car accident he was in had the ability to end his career. But with sheer will power, determination and endless efforts, the legend recovered and is back in the national XI. Of course it helps when the world's richest Board (BCCI) backs him to the hilt. They provided all the necessary infrastructure to aid in his recovery. But remember not every injured athlete is going to get the same treatment from the BCCI or your local team the way Rishabh did.

This is why you need to build your own support team. Look back at the "Networking Chapter" where I have outlined how to surround yourself with good physios, coaches, and well-wishers. These are the people who will bring you back on track with your recovery and rehab programs. Find a strong headed, good sports physiotherapist. And once you find him/her, build a long term relationship with them. They're going to be of a great help in getting you back on the field in time. Your support team will help you identify weaknesses or imbalances in your body. Whether you need Rehab, Prehab or massage therapy, these are the people who will help you in need.

Another disclaimer that I'd like to put in here, especially for athletes playing at the lower level, if you are injured during the off season, then inform only those you trust. You do not need to tell everyone about it. I say this, because at the lower level in sports there are high chances that although you might recover from your injury, your selectors or clubs around you might not take notice of you, because at the back of their minds, you are still nursing an injury. So the best course of action is to lay low and recover in your own time.

One must also remember the role that luck plays in injuries. Yes, you have to be lucky when it comes to injuries. Lucky enough to be injury free throughout your career (it's a bit of a stretch, but one can hope) or lucky enough to get injured but at the right time.

Let me explain this. If you get injured in the off season or at the end of the season, then you are lucky. There are many who get injured in the prime of the season and have to let go of playing for the remainder of the season.

Next, remember that injuries are a blessing not a curse.

If you work with sincerity and diligence on your injuries in your Rehab, doing all the exercises prescribed, follow the rest and recovery routine, you will come out stronger than before.

I know these lines might just sound very flowery and "motivational", so let me get down to the nitty gritty of Rehab.

REHAB

Rehabilitation (commonly known as rehab) is the process of responding to an injury by working on repairing, reconstructing, and restoring the affected joint, bone, muscle, tendon, ligament, or organ. The goal of rehab is not just healing but also ensuring that the injured area regains its strength, flexibility, and functionality to prevent future setbacks.

The rehab program depends on the type and severity of the injury:

- **Mild injuries (sprains, minor muscle tears)** – Require short-term rehab with rest, physiotherapy, and gradual strengthening exercises.

- **Moderate injuries (ligament sprains, muscle tears)** – Demand structured rehab with controlled mobility exercises, pain management, and progressive strengthening.

- **Severe injuries (ACL tears, fractures, dislocations, surgeries)** – Involve long-term rehab that may last months and require intensive physiotherapy, strength rebuilding, and sport-specific retraining.

If an athlete gets injured during the season, they often face a time crunch and may be forced to accelerate their rehab to return to competition. Then the only way forward is to bow your head down and dive into an intense Rehab plan. Appropriate rest and recovery time should be given priority over anything else. Do not think of what you are missing out on, look at the bigger picture and just focus on what your body needs from you at the moment. If you can do that, then by the time you walk down onto the field the next time, you will be a sharp and resilient player.

However, if the injury occurs during the off-season, the athlete has a better recovery window, allowing them to rebuild properly without the pressure of missing matches.

PREHAB

Prehabilitation (prehab) refers to preventive exercises and strategies designed to minimize the risk of injury. Instead of reacting to an injury (as in rehab), prehab focuses on proactive measures to strengthen weak areas, improve mobility, and enhance biomechanics to reduce injury susceptibility.

Prehab is primarily done in the off-season, as this is when athletes can focus on addressing underlying weaknesses, imbalances, or recurring niggles without the pressure of competition. It is particularly important for athletes who have a history of repeated injuries or who play high-impact sports with high injury risks (e.g., football, basketball, cricket, tennis).

A well-structured **prehab program** includes:

- **Recurring physical injuries** - As an athlete you are aware of any recurring pains, niggles or major injuries within your body. Focus on strengthening those muscles or proactively fixing those issues during your prehab program.

- **Strength training** – To reinforce muscles, tendons, and ligaments.

- **Mobility and flexibility exercises** – To improve range of motion and prevent stiffness.

- **Stability and balance training** – To enhance joint control and prevent awkward movements.

- **Sport-specific conditioning** – To prepare the body for the physical demands of competition.

By focusing on prehab, athletes can reduce injury risks, increase career longevity, and optimize performance during the season.

Another often unspoken aspect of injury management is the period of work you need to put in to stay in shape. There are a few chronic injuries that you have to work upon for the entire duration of your career. In case of bowlers, javelin throwers, and tennis players the rotator cuff takes a beating. Most of them have to keep working on it for the rest of their career, to play with the same intensity, in every match. Your rehab routine or the prescribed physio exercise have to become a natural part of your workout routine. Your discipline will keep you strong and help you keep going.

Mentality & Injury Management

Moving to the most important part of this chapter - "Mindset or Mentality in Injury Management". When dealing with an injury, especially one that demands prolonged recovery time and routine is tough. I have seen players who get so mentally bogged down that they think of calling it a day.

Injuries can hamper your mental well-being to an extent that it can put you off training out of the fear of getting injured again. The one thing to understand here is, you need to stick to your plan, no matter what. A warrior mindset can take you miles ahead. I suggest you read about this person called Hal Elrod. He came back from the brink of death and achieved amazing feats, only because,

a. He accepted the situation.

b. he trusted the process of recovery with a positive attitude.

c. He kept his head down and did the work.

None of the points from "a to c" above are optional, all must be implemented for optimal success in injury management.

Another example that comes to mind is that of Vinny Pazienza, a boxer who met with a car accident and broke his neck. Forget boxing, the doctors were certain that a slight jerk would snap his neck and kill him, but he worked hard and defied all odds to come back and win the world title. A movie was made about his life in 2016, called ***Bleed for This***. Go watch it.

A lot of times, you need to shut out all the noise in your brain and do the work. Follow the process, and be patient. Rome wasn't built in a day, remember.

And don't worry, I know, it is very natural to get disheartened, it's also very easy to get distraught due to injuries. Nevertheless, it is totally up to you, to get back on track, and become better and find a way around these situations. Setbacks are the way of life. Just like the matches you play, you win some, you lose some.

Make peace with pain. You are never going to be a hundred percent okay.an athlete needs to have a high pain threshold.there might be times when you have to enter the field with an injury because your team needs you.you will have to do it for the team. Even the best of athletes have a few niggles. You should know which ones you can perform with and which hinders your performance. Here enters the concept of Workload Management.

Workload Management

Workload Management is something you slowly come to grasp as you keep growing in your career and learn more about your body and identify its optimal performance levels. Your learnings about when you should be opting to rest and recover, and when you push through and perform on the field. Understanding your own body and mind is a key performance indicator that you shouldn't ignore. This has to be chalked out with reference to your game season, where you should be at your optimal best.

Managing workload includes how often you workout, how much do you practise, what intensity you practise, what splits you follow with regards to your strength and conditioning etc.

Another important aspect athletes ignore and need to pay attention with extreme focus is to NOT take unnecessary risks. Ignoring this can amplify your chances of getting injured.

Once you are a professional athlete, any sport other than your primary sport, goes out of the window. There are so many cricketers that get injured playing football due to the vast difference in nature of the two games. Such unnecessary risks are best avoided. There is a very thin line in being confident and being plain stupid. Stick to your chosen sport and work on everything necessary for that sport. Period.

If you know you are clumsy, learn to be aware of your surroundings. Be present in that moment, and not dilly dally here and there, engrossed in your own world. Being aware is an important step in being mentally strong. Calibrate your body like the ADAS (Advanced Driver Assistance System) sensors seen in today's cars.

Look out for your blind spots, slow down a little early when you see dangerous objects. Just bring your on-field awareness off field too.

The key to dealing with injuries is "Mind over matter". Learn to accept the pain, the loss of your peak fitness and the most cruel one "the loss of time". But remember that you are making a career in sports, one of the most unpredictable, unstable and unforgiving avenues in the world.

You must be tougher than the rest, you must have something that others don't and it is not just talent, it is all about your warrior mindset. Find strength to go on even when everything seems to be broken down, because no one will fight your battles for you. Don't forget what you are fighting for and you'll never lose against injuries!

Chapter XIII

Addictions

————— ❖ —————

*"Anything that leeches away your time and
focus from the game is an addiction."*

What stops an athlete from achieving greatness? What stops a cricketer from living up to his fullest potential? And no, I am not asking about external factors like selection or circumstances. I am asking about what goes wrong internally for an athlete that derails their career.

The answer is addiction.

Addictions come in all shapes and sizes, and they are like termites, destroying the athlete's capacity to perform slowly and steadily.

Most of the time, a sportsperson won't even notice that they are addicted to something. It might start off very casually, as a once-in-a-while thing, almost harmless. But if an addiction grows, it affects the player mentally and physically to a point where it negatively impacts their performance on the field.

This is the reason I feel we need to speak more openly and loudly about addictions. Addictions have destroyed the careers of highly talented sports stars in every type of sport known to man. I believe that if the upcoming generation of athletes is made aware of the dangers of addiction early on, we can hopefully reverse this trend, and more youngsters will have fulfilling careers.

First of all, let's understand what an addiction truly means.

According to Healthdirect Australia, the national virtual public health information service, ***"Addiction is when you have a strong physical or psychological need or urge to do something or use something. It is a dependence on a substance or activity even if you know that it causes you harm."***

The best part about this definition is that it no longer restricts addiction to dependence on 'substances' but expands it to include 'activities'. Because, in reality, addictions in the modern world are much more than just alcohol or drugs.

Now, I am going to explicitly name the addictions so as to not leave any ambiguity for my readers, including parents of athletes and the sports persons themselves.

Substance Addictions:

1. Alcohol

2. Nicotine or smoking

3. Tobacco in any form

4. Vaping or hookah

5. Drugs—marijuana, heroin, cocaine and other type of intoxicating drug

6. Any Performance Enhancing Drugs (PEDs)

Most likely, you are already aware of all or at least some of the above items that lead to substance addiction. If not, then you are aware now!

The addictions in this category from points 2 to 6 are a strict no-no. The items listed will ruin your body and mind. Alcohol is occasionally okay but never overdo it.

The second category of addictions is 'activity' based addictions. This category is a little tricky to define or make an exhaustive list of; still, we will try to cover the major ones in it.

1. Social media
2. Screen time
3. Over indulgence in food
4. Partying
5. Over socialising
6. Over training
7. Gambling

Most of these activities in themselves are not addictive and should not be treated as such. One should not completely swear off them except for gambling, just because you wish to become a great athlete or cricketer someday.

For example, screen time is unavoidable in today's day and age. So, I am not asking you to go back to the vintage Nokia phones or remove all laptops and tablets from your vicinity. Not at all. All I want you to do is learn to restrict your screen time to a bare minimum. Basically, learn to keep your exposure to any type of screen (outside of work) to less than 90 minutes every day, especially if you are pursuing an individual sport.

The basic principle that one should follow to avoid any activity-based addiction is 'Everything in moderation'. You need to stay in balance and do everything within healthy limits.

You are not expected to live life like a monk just because you chose to become a professional sportsperson. Don't let anyone tell you otherwise.

Let's go into a little more detail about the activities I have listed above.

- Social Media

  Social media is a double-edged sword. On the one hand, if fine-tuned and used productively, it can give you a wealth of insights from the world's biggest experts on any topic. On the other hand, if you allow the algorithm to dictate your feed and voluntarily keep looking for stuff that is just entertainment or cringe, then you will be stuck in a loop of consumption for just a fake dopamine high. That is dangerous. So, learn to curate your social media content to your advantage and restrict the amount of time you spend on these apps.

- Screen time. I've already explained my views in the example above.

- Overindulgence in food

  As an athlete, your body is your biggest asset. Food is your fuel. The right type of food at the right time can work wonders for you. But what if your desire to eat starts altering your food choices from healthy to unhealthy? What if you start eating for your taste buds more than what your body needs? If you regularly choose fast food over healthy food, restaurant-made items over home-cooked meals and your diet is dictated by your cravings, then, my dear friend, you are in deep trouble. Learn to consciously make healthy food choices at least 90% of the time and enjoy your Vada Pavs and burgers during the remaining 10%.

- Partying

Personally, my thoughts on partying are not in line with the 'everything in moderation' principle. In this case, I believe 'the less, the better'. Partying puts you in situations where a lot of things are beyond your control. You are in environments like pubs and bars, where there is a very low possibility of anything 'good' happening.

Look at what happened with Jesse Ryder, the Kiwi cricketer. He got into a scuffle with two men in a bar. Later, he was attacked by those men and was almost fatally injured. This attack and injury almost ended his cricket career completely.

Ben Stokes, England's exceptional all-rounder, was being a good Samaritan and was standing up for two gay men in a Bristol bar who were being verbally abused by two hooligans. This led to a fight where Ben Stokes struck the culprits and was later arrested by the UK police. He was dropped from the National Team and lost his vice-captaincy. He suffered a lot mentally before being absolved from this case.

There are many such examples where athletes have been injured during partying or have had unpleasant experiences in general.

Hence, my advice: tread with caution when partying.

- Over socialising

Humans are social creatures by nature. Having a group of friends is a great support system, especially in an unpredictable career like sports. But just spending every evening or every free day hanging out with your friends endlessly is counterproductive to your career. If you get sucked into the environment of just 'chilling' all the time, then when will you get into the 'zone' of preparation and performance fully? So make time for friends but not at the cost of your career.

- Overtraining

  This is a tough one. Most players will first of all raise the question, "Is there anything like overtraining?" Yes, there is. Athletes get a high on training. They feel at the top of the world at the end of a training session. Before long, they start chasing this feeling at every session. They ignore their body's demand for rest or neglect signs of niggles because they need that high. This is a red flag. Stop yourself in time to preserve your body and your mental health.

- Gambling

  A player's life is full of financial uncertainties. It is, therefore, tempting to make some quick money through gambling. Many athletes fall prey to the addiction of gambling. Sometimes, it is the urgency with which they need money; sometimes, it is to help them continue on their cricket journey. The promise of winning large sums of money gets many athletes into deep debt with gambling.

Another money-related problem is players starting to borrow funds from friends and family to fuel other addictions and lifestyle choices. They become habituated to regularly asking for money, switching circles where they ask for money, and paying back some of it from time to time so as not to be totally cut off.

Money is a powerful resource, and the lack of it can be extremely frustrating. But it is important to completely avoid addiction to either gambling or borrowing money. Neither of these addictions will help you in becoming a better player or a good family man.

Lastly, there is a delicate point that I haven't listed above, but I would like to address. Everyone has the need for physical intimacy and relationships. Athletes have fantastic physical strength and stamina; they also tend to have higher testosterone levels compared to non-athletes. This naturally means a higher sex drive.

There are many sportspeople, irrespective of gender, who have let their physical needs get the better of them. They let this desire take control, and this may lead to ill effects in their personal lives as well as on their performance. I don't wish to take any moral stand here; I just want you to make informed decisions.

Addictions have the power to break your career as well as your personal life. People who give in to addictions make their own lives hell and make their families suffer, too.

It is better to steer clear of addictions and proactively monitor your habits, your company, and how you spend your time. The more conscious you are, the better your choices.

Bonus: Player Analysis

Diego Maradona

Footballer Diego Maradona is one of the biggest legends in the world of football. He put Argentinian football on the map and inspired generations of footballers from all across the globe.

If you've never witnessed how Diego Maradona warmed up before a game, a quick search on YouTube will leave you in awe.

His unparalleled ball control was mesmerising, something no one before or after has been able to replicate.

With 41 goals for Argentina, Maradona is undeniably one of the greatest football players of all time. His crowning achievement came in the 1986 World Cup, where he almost single-handedly led Argentina to victory, cementing his status as the nation's greatest footballing hero before Lionel Messi rose to prominence.

However, Maradona's life off the field was as turbulent as his performances were brilliant. He lived a highly controversial life, including a notorious ban for cocaine consumption, a full-blown addiction that not only affected his game but also cut his career short. Tragically, his struggles tarnished his legacy, a legacy built on raw talent and moments of footballing genius that the world will never forget.

Chapter XIV

Admiration V. Hero Worship

*"Your role models have found their
own way to the top. You must, too."*

We Indians are a sentimental lot, and more so in two cases—Films and cricket. In these two avenues, our sentiments often turn from adoration to hero worship. You will see this in the case of Sachin Tendulkar, the God of Cricket, Amitabh Bachchan or the Big B of Hindi movies, Rajnikanth, the Thalaivaa of Tamil cinema, and so many more examples across generations, emerging from different states and cities of India. Once Indians turn a cricketer or a film star into a 'hero', he/she becomes a larger-than-life persona, a persona that commands fame, attention, and influence in the minds of the masses.

This trajectory is what attracts a lot of young players to sports. They seek a similar amount of success, riches, and the intoxicating effects of fame. That shallow attraction for the 'by-product' of good cricket is what I find dangerous.

In this chapter, I am going to discuss the difference between admiring a sports star and worshipping them blindly. Throughout the course of this chapter, I will make a conscious effort to show you the side effects of hero worship, and I will also show you what admiration can do to improve your game.

Who Are Your Heroes?

Sporting heroes are those who have given phenomenal performances on the field, won laurels for the country, and are dedicated to their game. These players make a name for themselves with their achievements, but soon, they also start becoming famous for how they live their lives, what they buy, what they endorse, and even who they marry.

For example, MS Dhoni, one of the greatest captains in Indian cricketing history, first came into the public eye with his outstanding performance against Pakistan. Even then, what became a highlight alongside his performance was his unique hairstyle. As his fame grew, more and more people started noticing his other passions, such as his collection of bikes and cars. The nation suddenly had more bike lovers than before, and the 'Dhoni' hairstyle was also quite popular.

This is just one example, fresh in public memory. I could give you hundreds more like this, and the story will remain the same, performances followed by their personality and lifestyle choices.

Now this is where I want you, the athlete to start distinguishing yourself from the non-athletes. It is totally fine for the non-athletes to emulate sport stars for everything other than their craft. But you as an athlete need to bring attention to their skill, their dedication, and their work ethic.

Inspiration vs. Worship

As an athlete, although the lifestyle and the personality of the hero are very enchanting, you cannot fall for it!

Your focus should be on his/her athleticism and their ability to perform in different circumstances. Let us look at Virat Kohli, the GOAT of cricket, not just Indian cricket but the global sport of cricket. The man is a rockstar on the field. He is the master of run chases; he can sustain immense pressure and is committed to his team's vision from the first ball to the last one of the match.

He is also aggressive on the field. He abuses after getting a wicket. His tattoos are flashy, and his personality is loud.

What do you take from him? Do you take his flashy tattoos, or do you take how he fiercely chases down targets? Do you take his abusive traits, or do you take his intensity during practice and during performance?

As an athlete, look for the qualities in the hero that have made him so admirable. If you are idolising Virat Kohli, then here's a list of things that you can learn from him:

- His commitment to fitness. He has literally turned his life around to become one of the fittest athletes in the world. He is extremely strict about his nutrition, follows an intense workout regimen and is always there for training sessions.be it on the ground or inside the gym.

- There's a reason he is known as the greatest chase master in the history of cricket. He has the ability to read the game, calculate, and plan his strategy with precision to win the game, and he has done this for more than a decade. How does he do it? How he manages to keep things so simple amidst all the chaos on the pitch are the questions one must find answers to.

- His speed on the field while running between the wickets or fielding helps the team in ways you cannot think. He saves runs while fielding and while batting he converts ones into twos. Giving his side an advantage of 15 to 20 runs every game. Which is a lot.

- His energy on the field be it batting, bowling or fielding inspires and lifts the entire team in testing situations.

- His ability to introspect. Like any great player in history, Virat has seen his fair share of criticism and bad form. However, he has the ability to look inward and work to improve his weaknesses. He believes he's the best, but he also knows when to be humble and put his head down and grind, and that is what helps him grow. The best example of this is his 2024 T20 World Cup final knock.

- His devotion to Team India. Virat has gone from being a newcomer to a captain and back to being a senior player in the team. He has accepted the shift with immense grace and remained devoted to the betterment of the team above his individual records.

- His ability to adapt, evolve and overcome. from being the ultra-aggressive alpha on the field to becoming a much milder version of himself without letting go of the hunger and passion to win games, to elongate his playing career is admirable.

If your idol is Virat Kohli, then this is what you should be imbibing from him and not how much following he has on Instagram or where he goes on holiday. That is a by-product of success. If he stops working hard, he will eventually lose it all, and he knows this more than anyone else.

I will name a few more great players and what you should be learning from them as an athlete.

1. Saurav Ganguly: His aggressive leadership, coupled with his ability to manage a team of big names while nurturing young talent, gifted Indian cricket with gems like Harbhajan Singh, Zaheer Khan, Yuvraj Singh, Virender Sehwag, Ashish Nehra, and Mohammad Kaif. Ganguly inspired the team to believe in their greatness, even when facing formidable opponents like Australia. His strategic acumen as a captain ushered in a new and transformative era for Indian cricket.

2. Rahul Dravid: His unwavering commitment to perfecting his technique and adhering to the process in every game set him apart. Dravid's exceptional concentration, coupled with the mental toughness and grit to endure on the pitch for hours, earned him the reputation of being 'The Wall', especially during the most challenging situations.

3. Cristiano Ronaldo: His tireless resolve to maintain a rigorous routine year after year, never taking his innate talent for granted, even at the age of 40, is a testament to his dedication. By consistently performing at the highest level for every team he represents, Ronaldo continues to prove he is one of the greatest footballers of all time. His ability to foster team spirit and lead by example further cements his legacy as an extraordinary athlete and leader.

4. Kobe Bryant: Always studying, always learning, always practising, a relentless pursuit of excellence defines him. Bryant's almost obsessive drive to outshine everyone, whether teammates or opponents, fuels his determination to stay one step ahead of everyone on the court.

5. Rohit Sharma: How to be a selfless and approachable leader, Sharma exemplifies this by prioritising the team's success over personal achievements, often sacrificing opportunities to set individual records for the greater good of the team.

These are just some examples. For every great player, you will find the key to success hidden in his/her qualities. Think of your sporting idols, list their qualities, and try to imbibe them into your life.

The Pitfalls of Blind Hero Worship

- Mimicry

  A common mistake you might make on this path is to try to copy your hero's playing style. Don't try to imitate Sachin Tendulkar's stance or the way Jasprit Bumrah bowls. If you try copying your idols as they are, then you will lose your originality as a player.

  Never be a 'Ctrl + C' to 'Ctrl + V' player. If you start on the journey of mimicking the style of play, that is a point of no return for your own style of play. You will be doing a disservice to your talent if you blindly copy cricketing greats. You will not go very far in your cricket career based on a 'copy-paste' style. Remember, there is already a player who is the OG, and you will merely be a cheap second copy. Instead, retain your originality and work on your technique.

- Herd Mentality

  The next pitfall arises from the 'herd' mentality. Many times, players choose their idols based on what's trending. You will simply follow the herd; if their current hero is Hardik Pandya, then so is yours. If their favourite bowler is Jasprit Bumrah, then so is yours. This is definitely a blunder on your part.

At any given point in time, the world is full of amazing players in every sport (thank God for that!). And some of these players are at the pinnacle of their success and fame. Most of them are the ones who are hugely hero-worshipped. But I want you, the athlete, to look beyond that success and popular opinion. I want you to seek relatability in your heroes. You can become a fan of multiple players and legends, but you must choose your idols very carefully. Seek out someone who has a thought process or personality similar to yours.

If you are a laid-back or carefree person on the field, and being like that on the field helps you perform better, then you could choose Rohit Sharma or Lionel Messi to be your idol, since they are complementary to your innate nature. Similarly, if you are someone who thrives on intensity and aggression, then maybe Rafael Nadal or Zlatan Ibrahimovic is a better fit for you. But if this choice is not helping you perform better then reconsider your choice and find a better-suited role model.

- Heroes vs Legends

Often, I have seen the new generation hero worship simply based on one thing, who is at the top of their game. This factor is an important factor, no doubt, but it cannot be the only determining factor in your choice. There are a vast number of athletes who may never achieve the amount of success or feats that a #1 player in the sport may achieve. But they are still good athletes in their own right. Take someone like Suresh Raina or Ravindra Jadeja, for example. They are brilliant fielders, great batsmen, and full of team spirit.

Suresh Raina was the first cricketer to score a century in all three formats. He holds the record for the most catches taken in the IPL, with 107 catches in his name. Raina has been a useful off-break bowler for the Indian team during his career.

Similarly, Ravindra Jadeja, the left-arm off-spinner and a crucial batsman in the lower order, has proven his mettle with both the bat and ball time and again. His reputation with fielding is so outstanding that the moment a ball travels towards him, the batsmen rethink their plans of scoring a run. Jadeja has complemented the middle order with good knocks and the bowling unit with his skill.

Both of these men have contributed to the success of the Indian Cricket Team. But both of them will never achieve the level of fame or success that Sachin or Yuvraj commanded. So this shouldn't instantly disqualify them from becoming your heroes. If you find them to be a good fit for your personality and your aspirations, then go ahead and idolise them. Do not depend on public opinion to choose your hero.

- Wrong Expectations

If you idolise someone and work in exactly the way they did, you might start expecting your journey to be similar to theirs. This is a setup for disappointment and heartbreak. Your journey is fully yours; it cannot be a replication of someone else's path. Your heroes are human, too, and they are going to make mistakes on the way. Don't expect them to be perfect and constantly at the peak of their performance. Never set your expectations in such a manner.

How Can Your Hero Help You?

Now, this is the interesting part of the chapter. Does hero worship really help with your skill? Does it help you in becoming a better player?

Yes, most definitely, it does.

Your hero is teaching you big life lessons unconsciously. They are imparting you with the wisdom they have probably learnt the hard way. They are giving you the tools to become an amazing athlete while shaping their own career along the way.

A good hero will teach you what it takes to play in the big leagues. They will teach you:

- Discipline

- Dedication to your skill

- Emotional flexibility in the toughest situations

- Maturing as a person and player

- How to handle failures, bad form, injuries and setbacks

- How fickle fame and the love of fans could be (case in point– Hardik Pandya)

Before we conclude this chapter, here are my book/video recommendations for you and why you should read/watch them:

1. A Century Is Not Enough–Sourav Ganguly

   He portrays what it takes to be a mentally tough player, leader, and a human being to thrive in sports and life.

2. The Mamba Mentality: How I Play–Kobe Bryant

   This is a technical book on basketball. Kobe has detailed how he studied his opponents and formed strategies on how to beat them on the court mentally, physically, and technically.

3. Kobe Bryant interview with Patrick David

   This interview is a revelation. Kobe opens up about his strategic craft of planning and working to become the best basketball player in the world. He reveals his thought process. His ability to look at the big picture while working on the smaller pieces of the jigsaw puzzle is incredible.

4. Beckham, the Netflix series, is based on David Beckham's life.

    This limited-episode series is the perfect example of how an athlete should carry himself through criticism, unfavourable situations, and bad management while continuing to be a thorough professional.

5. The Last Dance on Netflix - Michael Jordan

    In this series, you will learn about what self-belief can do for an athlete. Michael's self-belief and drive to become the greatest athlete have fuelled his career and achievements like no other.

In short, a good hero, the right hero for you, will make you a better person and a better athlete. Their legacy is far greater than the numbers stacked against their name. Their legacy is more ethereal and leaves a mark in the lives of their fans and followers forever.

Bonus: Player Analysis

Tiger Woods

With 15 major championships, Tiger Woods is undeniably one of the greatest golfers of all time. If you set statistics aside and focus purely on skill, he is arguably the best golfer the world has ever seen. Woods achieved nearly everything in his sport, solidifying his place in history.

However, his life off the course became a source of embarrassment for many of the fans who once cheered for him. Despite his immense talent and numerous accolades, personal controversies prevented him from fully realising his potential as the greatest golfer ever.

This raises an important question: as an athlete, would you idolise someone like Tiger Woods? If you do, how discerning are you in understanding what to emulate from their lives?

It's worth noting that both Woods and other athletes with troubled pasts often reflect the hardships they experienced as children, learning behaviours from their early environments. While it's easy for us to criticise them, it's important to remember that they are human. Yet, their personal choices and actions make it difficult to view them as role models.

Every athlete faces challenges, whether financial, familial, or mental. True role models are those who excel both on and off the field, maintaining integrity despite the obstacles they encounter. An athlete is, above all, a human being, and it's their character that ultimately defines their legacy.

Chapter XV

Fielding

————————— ❖ —————————

"If you want to see how committed a cricketer is, observe him field."

On any day and at any stage of cricket, if you are preparing in the nets or on the field, your preparation should be deemed incomplete if you aren't doing fielding practice.

Fielding is the most underrated activity in cricket. At the local-level, everyone, including the coaches, ignored fielding.

This callous attitude towards fielding often angers me to the core. I staunchly believe that 'fielding is the best defence strategy for a team'.

Why Fielding Is an Essential Skill?

Good fielding can help you win matches, and bad fielding will result in significant losses. Good fielding when you are bowling first ensures that the target remains reasonable; you support your bowlers by saving runs and taking catches. This, in turn, helps your batsmen because they have a lower target to chase and a little less pressure. When you field well as the team bowling second, you maintain a tight grip on the game. You help in keeping the batsmen under pressure. Good fielding efforts from you will show everyone how ready you are or how committed you are to the match you're playing.

We all know what happens when the team doesn't field well, matches slip away, runs trickle out of control, batsmen get lifelines with every catch dropped, and the game is all but lost.

There have been so many close matches that either team has managed to win solely because they fielded well. Another important point of observation that comes to mind is that fielding is contagious, whether good or bad. Once a team member begins to field well, the energy catches on and once you see team members midfield or drop catches, it plays on your mind too. I have seen this happen countless times both at the local-level and the international level.

Fielding is the most selfless activity you will do in a team game like cricket. Good fielding has helped elevate the career of so many bowlers because good fielding ultimately shows up as 'lower runs conceded per over' and 'wickets taken' in the stats of the bowler. This is one act that gives your teammates a push in the right direction and will help you cement your bond with them.

Fielding As a Skill - Non-Negotiable

My attitude towards fielding is very clear, it is a non-negotiable requirement if you want to succeed as a cricketer. You must spend time and make an effort to improve your fielding skills every single day.

Ganguly and Dhoni gave importance to improving Indian fielding, which helped us successfully win important series and tournaments.

Sometimes, I feel cricketers forget that while batting and bowling happen in a one-on-one fashion, fielding is only a team activity. Every person on the team has to play in some position and contribute towards the goal. Then how can something that is so essential to the very essence of a team sport be ignored?

Fielding is a way of showing respect for your teammates' efforts. A good fielder supports the bowling unit, and a bad fielder brings it down. It is your job, therefore, to do the bare minimum and at least become a safe fielder for your team to show respect for the bowling unit.

Fielding Practice 101

As you head for training and make your daily checklist, ensure that you keep a slot in your schedule as well as the checklist dedicated to fielding.

There are five important basic elements of fielding:

1. Catching
2. Ground fielding
3. Throwing (keeper/bowler/stumps)
4. Diving
5. Fielding and catching at different positions

Select one aspect that you will be focusing on for that day and train for it. Keep rotating this cycle to ensure that you don't backslide on your fielding skills.

Work on the foundation of your fielding practice and then upgrade your skills for the big leagues.

The advanced elements that should be incorporated into your fielding practice are:

1.   Red ball and white ball fielding practice.

2.   Fielding based on the conditions (ground and weather).

3.   Specialised position practice.

4.   Visualisation.

5.   Fielding under pressure.

Let's go a little more in-depth on the advanced elements of fielding.

1.   Red ball & white ball fielding practice:

Professional cricket is played with two different balls, the red leather ball and the white leather ball. The red ball is used in Test cricket and First-Class cricket, while the white ball is used for ODIs and T20 matches.

Both of these balls bring their own set of challenges for the fielders. The red ball has a natural polish and holds its condition longer than the white ball.

The white ball, on the other hand, has undergone more chemical processing and discolours faster. However, the additional chemical processing also makes it harder.

Nuances like this affect how the ball wears out during the innings, how it travels, and even the visibility during high catches. As a fielder, you must practise with both balls in varying conditions. The more you practise, the less 'surprised' you will be on the field.

2. Fielding based on the conditions

As a cricketer, you are already aware of the different variables that affect the game. Two of the biggest such variables are the weather and the ground conditions.

The weather conditions deeply affect the game. When it's windy, your ball is either going to travel farther or dip according to the direction of the wind, and you need to be able to judge the direction of the wind to know how the ball is travelling and react accordingly. If it is rainy or overcast and the weather has more dew, then the ball is wet, making it heavier than usual. If the weather is cold, then the ball stings more when it hits your hand, and you need to be prepared for that; otherwise, you will field half-heartedly and make more mistakes.

As a fielder, it is important to build your fielding around the weather conditions. Use the weather to your advantage and practice in different conditions to get used to them.

Similarly, the ground conditions are also important, especially when you are playing local-level cricket and the grounds are small or badly kept. This will affect your fielding performance. In such situations, you should adopt a more defensive approach rather than an attacking approach that you would normally follow in good ground conditions.

On dry and hard ground, the ball will bounce higher and travel faster. On soft and damp ground, the ball moves slower, but you might skid while stopping the ball or trying to catch it. A rough and uneven ground, mostly seen in local-level cricket, makes fielding risky, and hence, players must stay alert to avoid injuries.

Each and every aspect of the weather and the ground conditions is going to make an impact on the ultimate split-second reaction of being able to stop the ball or catch the ball in time. Therefore, prepare yourself mentally and physically to field in all types of conditions.

3. Specialised position practice

Specialist fielders in cricket play a very important role, especially when it comes to supporting the bowlers and getting crucial wickets. The team depends on these fielding positions to put pressure on the batsmen and mentally dominate the game as well as physically.

The Indian Cricket Team, for a very long time, did not pay much attention to fielding. Our fielders were mediocre, and we were one of the weakest fielding sides in the world.

When Captain Sourav Ganguly took over the reins of Team India, he began building the young guns like Yuvraj Singh, Mohammed Kaif and Suresh Raina to become specialist fielders.

We have already covered the challenges of specialist positions in the advanced fielding section.

These positions hold a high weightage and need special training, since your reflexes need to be sharp, your technique on point, and your intensity should remain high for the entire innings.

I don't need to remind you of what Surya Kumar Yadav performed at the long off position in the finals of the T20 World Cup 2024, he literally caught the trophy for us with sheer skill and quick thinking!

Earlier, Captains used to hide their weaker fielders in so-called 'safe fielding positions' like Third Man, Fine Leg, and Deep Square Leg. But now, with the way cricket has evolved, no positions are safe positions. Especially if you are playing T20, where batsmen can hit in any direction, and you ought to be ready to defend your team.

After Sourav Ganguly, MS Dhoni carried forward this legacy and shaped the mindset of the upcoming generation to become ruthless fielders.

Ravindra Jadeja is the perfect example of a ruthless fielder. He has mastered the art of fielding. Put him in any position, and the team is assured of defence and catches. His lightning-fast run-outs have put fear in the minds of batsmen.

At the highest levels of cricket, if you don't perform as a fielder, you are out of the picture. There is no leeway for poor fielders. If you aspire to play at this level, then you should work towards it from today.

The main positions that are covered under this are:

- Slip
- Gully
- Point
- Cover
- Long-on and long off (in white ball cricket)

The reaction time in these positions is literally split seconds. Most of the time, the fielding in these positions is 'do or die' – one mistake will cost your team, and the right fielding will earn you respect among your teammates.

Every position here will require a different type of fielding practice because the way shots are played and the ball travels is drastically different for each of these positions.

For example, the slip specialist stands next to the wicketkeeper and has to be ready for catches of the edge, which travel at lightning speed, along with laterally moving balls to stop potential boundaries.

A fielder at point, on the other hand, needs to have good anticipation of the possible shots and be ready for run-out opportunities.

Depending on the specialist position you are practising for, your training should vary. Precise training will give you an edge on the field and instil fear in the minds of the opposing team.

4. Visualisation

The challenges of fielding are intense. It is not possible for you as a player to train for each scenario and condition. There are going to be many matches where you will have to learn fielding on the job.

This is where visualisation will play a vital role for you. By mentally rehearsing scenarios and techniques, fielders can enhance their focus, reaction times, and overall effectiveness.

Visualising the ball's trajectory from the bowler to the batsman and anticipating possible edges or deflections will help fielders in reacting more quickly. Visualising diving, sliding, and catching movements can improve muscle memory, leading to faster and more precise physical responses during the game.

Use visualisation to strengthen your confidence as a fielder. For example, Suryakumar Yadav or SKY, caught the most important catch of his career at Long Off. Do you think he caught it just like that? The answer is no, he did not. He must've practised this scenario in his visualisation a hundred times before. All he had to do was use this practice, keep his nerves calm and take the catch. Split-second decisions usually go right when you practice them in your head and then on the field. And this is precisely why we went to the streets to celebrate the World Cup win after 13 years.

5. Fielding under pressure

Fielding under pressure is one of the toughest things to do in the match. More so, if you are an inexperienced or out-of-touch fielder, your reflexes will be slower, you won't be able to anticipate the ball fast enough, and this will result in sloppy midfields and mistakes.

To avoid this situation, whenever you train for fielding, try to create pressure test scenarios in your mind. For example, if you are practising catches, then imagine that one catch/run-out missed is equal to losing the match. Putting yourself in such situations again and again will mentally toughen you up for the real game.

When you do your fielding practice, remember there is nothing extraordinarily different about this. The method for this training is the same as any aspect of your training; watch the ball and follow the process all the time. If you keep doing this repeatedly with increasing levels of challenge, you will eventually get better at it.

At the lower levels of cricket, you will realise that your coaching staff doesn't have a dedicated 'fielding coach'. This speaks volumes about the importance given to fielding in our cricketing infrastructure.

If you are training at the domestic level, then grab your teammates or your coach and work on the parameters I have mentioned above. Nobody will probably encourage you to make such an effort in fielding practice, but it will pay off spectacularly in the long run for your career.

Spectacular Fielders of Cricket:

The sport of cricket has seen some spectacular and exceptional fielders over the years. As a cricket student, I will make a few recommendations for you. Go and watch these fielding legends to feel inspired and learn from their technique, alertness, sharp reflexes, and commitment:

- Martin Guptill
- Brendon McCullum
- Ravindra Jadeja
- Paul Collingwood
- Yuvraj Singh
- Mohammed Kaif
- Suresh Raina
- Rahul Dravid
- Jacques Kallis
- Mark Waugh
- Ricky Ponting
- Glen Maxwell
- Steve Smith
- Glen Phillips
- James Anderson
- Tim Southee

You will observe that most of the best fielders are batsmen, however I have added James Anderson and Tim Southee to the list, because in spite of being fast bowlers they are exceptional fielders and deserve a mention here. In today's cricket there's no running away from the fact that a bowler has to be a good fielder.

Watch the ball, catch the ball!

Keep it simple, and keep it consistent.

Chapter XVI

Plan B

—— ❖ ——

*"Life is unpredictable. When the ship is sinking,
you don't jump into the water. You will drown.
You jump into the lifeboat."*

You may see some great stories in sports where an athlete came from a humble background and turned things around for himself, but there are a thousand other stories of talented athletes who lost their path and their careers due to the unpredictable nature of the game because they were plain unlucky, weren't ready for the downfall, or did not have a plan B in place. Do not be that athlete. Not everyone can become Yashasvi Jaiswal, Cristiano Ronaldo, or LeBron James.

If you are someone who says any of the following:

- "I don't have a Plan B; it's do or die."
- "If Plan A doesn't work, try again."
- "There is no Plan B for passion."
- Etc. etc. etc.

Read on… I have news for you…

If this is the type of advice you've received from the sporting fraternity, and you are ready to follow it blindly, then I am going to stop you right now. Let me shake you and wake you up to reality. This whole 'you shouldn't have a Plan B if you are committed enough' is great for movies and speeches.

In real life, you should ALWAYS have a Plan B! Especially when you are dedicating your life to one of the most uncertain professions on the planet.

Sports are truly unpredictable. One day, you are up, and everything seems to be going your way, and the next day, you might be injured, which could be the end of your career. This is just one of a million possible scenarios.

So if you are putting everything on the line for a career like this, isn't it prudent for you to have a well-thought-out Plan B?

Why Should You Have a Plan B?

I know that just stating that sports are unpredictable isn't convincing enough for you to consider having a plan B.

So, I'll go further and share some bitter truths. I have seen many good, decent players struggle financially in life because they never had a Plan B in place, and Plan A didn't work out at the level they expected it to be. I have seen athletes who don't have a roof over their heads because they can't afford it. Many, many families have been destroyed because athletes were delusional and arrogant and refused to work on creating a stable livelihood for their loved ones. I don't even want to begin talking about what borrowing money and drinking to drown your sorrows does to your family.

This is a stark and unforgiving reality for many slightly successful and unsuccessful athletes. I don't want YOU to ever end up in this position, hence this chapter and hence my warning.

Who Should Have a Plan B?

If you are a sportsperson coming from a humble background, then you should definitely have a Plan B. In my observation, people who come from a lower middle class background or underprivileged classes cannot afford to have a Plan B and hence they don't give it a thought.

On the other hand, the rich or the elite don't need to have a Plan B since they are already well-off.

The middle class most likely has thought of a Plan B, but it might not be concrete and won't strategise on how to best implement it until the very last moment.

In my opinion, everyone up to the middle class should have a Plan B because their lifestyle and family depend on them to be financially stable. The elite may have a Plan B but don't necessarily need one since a shortage of money or income is not an issue for them. So they can figure out what to do if sports don't work out in their own sweet time.

When Should You Start Contemplating Plan B?

When age group cricket ends and if you have not made it to the National Team/First-Class cricket, then you should start contemplating Plan B.

Age group cricket acts like a safety net, allowing you to progress without fear. But when that safety net is taken off, you might start panicking; this will eventually affect your game.

If at the end of age group cricket, you haven't made it to the highest stage of cricket or at least First-Class cricket, then begin working on your Plan B simultaneously because this will be your new safety net.

A safety net is not going to choke you or stop you from pursuing your ambition of being in the National XI. It will, in fact, have the exact opposite effect. It will give you the freedom and peace of mind to chase your dreams with confidence and ease.

Look at Saurabh Netrawalkar as a shining example of a man with a Plan B! When he realised that his future in the Indian Cricket Team was not shaping up, he took the difficult decision to temporarily pause cricket and complete his engineering. He went on to pursue his Masters from Cornell University. Saurabh landed a great job at Oracle and finally found the financial freedom to go after cricket, too! His performance in the USA cricket team stood out in the 2024 T20I World Cup, and now he might just play in the IPL.

This is what life can offer you if you have a Plan B. Imagine the pride his family feels in his achievements in both cricketing and tech. Imagine the peace of mind he has, not having to worry about where the next paycheck is going to come from or whether or not he will be able to afford a new home or car!

What Should Be Your Plan B?

This is a tough question to ask yourself on its own. We will instead break it down into smaller analytical questions.

Sit down with a pen and paper and ponder deeply over what I am about to ask you next:

- What are your biggest concerns or fears about your post-sport career?

- What are your hobbies and interests outside of your sport?

- What skills have you developed through your sports career that could be transferable to other fields?

- What is your highest level of education as of now?

- Are you open to pursuing further education in your field of interest?

- Are there any fields or industries you are particularly interested in exploring?

- Have you gained any work experience outside of your sport? If yes, did you enjoy the work you were doing, and would you like to consider it part of your Plan B?

- Does your sport have a future in your country of residence? (You may be brilliant at your sport, but if your nation doesn't have enough infrastructure or support from the Ministry of Sports/ other government bodies, then your future within it is limited)

- Where do you stand financially as of now? (Be honest with yourself)

- How much money does your current lifestyle cost? How much would you need to earn to maintain the same lifestyle?

- Are you ready to work on personality development or soft skills development to further your career growth?

As you answer these questions, you will begin to see your Plan B outline more clearly.

While you think about these questions, I would like you to consider some pointers to guide you in the right direction:

1. Education is extremely important, and having a graduate degree is the bare minimum you should possess, even as a sportsperson.

2. Luck plays a vital role in shaping or breaking the careers of athletes. Always remember to factor in 1% of luck in your dreams and ambitions.

3. Sporting careers as it is not as long as traditional 9–5 jobs. Most athletes retire in their mid-30s. Thus, even if you become a successful athlete you will still need a Plan B for the next stage of your life.

4. Your Plan B should be set in motion at least 1 year in advance (2 would be better) of your own last given deadline.

5. Be ready to evolve or further develop your Plan B as life throws new opportunities your way.

6. Your own lifestyle and your family's comfort are your responsibility, so take them seriously.

At the end of this exercise, I hope you can clearly envision your Plan B and when and how you will execute it. Begin your preparations (education, finances, skill development, etc.) early on. This will give you peace of mind and the confidence to be skilled both on the field and off it. Your Plan B might not necessarily take you away from your sport. In fact, it could complement and help you elevate yourself in your sport.

How?

Well, some career options at the top of my mind are as follows:

1. Skill Coach
2. Strength & Conditioning Coach
3. Physiotherapist
4. Sports Nutritionist
5. Sports Psychologist
6. Talent Scout Manager
7. Sports Management

Do note that these options would require some specific education and certifications. Research the area you would prefer and the specific conditions they need you to fulfil, and get it done. This will help your game as well.

Most importantly, never look at your Plan B with even a tinge of negativity. Your Plan B is the insurance policy you take out, where you pay the premium on time and hope to God that you never have to actually use it. However, during tough times, this same insurance policy might mitigate the damages and help you in building a new life.

At the end of the day, life is not a 'movie' where everything will work out exactly the way the hero wants it to. Life is not always fair, and not everyone gets a fairytale ending.

If a time comes when you have to switch gears to execute your Plan B, do so with grace and your head held high. There is nothing wrong with building a different career path outside of your sporting career. You are doing the right thing for your own future and your loved ones.

A true athlete will remain one in spirit, even when they aren't 'professionals' anymore. Your discipline, grit, and work ethic will ensure that you become successful in your Plan B as well.

Your Plan B is not a sign of weakness; it is an indicator of having the courage to pursue your dreams on your own terms.

Bonus: Player Analysis

Hardy Sandhu

Many may not be aware that before becoming one of the top Punjabi singers in the country, Hardy Sandhu was a talented fast bowler who represented India U19, sharing the field with cricket stars like Rohit Sharma and Shikhar Dhawan.

Like many athletes, Hardy faced heartbreak in his sporting career when injuries derailed his cricketing aspirations. However, instead of dwelling on his misfortune, he had a Plan B in place, one rooted in his other passion and talent: music. Recognising his potential as a singer, he shifted his focus and began carving a new path for himself in the music industry.

Through determination and perseverance, Hardy transformed his life, and today, his chart-topping numbers are celebrated across the nation. His journey serves as an inspiring reminder for athletes and individuals alike to have a Plan B— one aligned with their skills and passions— to navigate unforeseen challenges and create new opportunities for success.

Chapter XVII

Mahoul

---

*"Your intentions don't matter.
Perception is reality."*

This is by far one of the most powerful quotes I have ever read in my life, and it is 100% the truth, especially in the life of an athlete. People's perception builds your 'Mahoul' in the sporting world. When I use the word 'Mahoul', I mean an intangible element, where your reputation or an environment, either conducive or destructive for you, is built by the opinions of people around you.

Everyone, in every field, is affected by the 'Mahoul' around them. All types of professionals will face the consequences of people's perceptions about them, both positive and negative. Isn't that why the old Hindi song, 'kuch toh log kahenge, logon ka kaam hain kehna' is so famous and often quoted when one suffers due to the Mahoul created around them.

If you are in any other field outside of sports, I would suggest living by the song's philosophy, which basically means, 'Don't be bothered by what people say about you'.

However, if you are an athlete, cricket player, or any kind of sportsperson, then let me warn you: this song is not for us! Our careers are shaped by our Mahoul, what people say about us, how they view us, and what it is about us that they strongly like or dislike. I am not saying this on a whim.

Let me prove it to you objectively. When you play a match (in this example, I am taking a small, local-level match), there are many people on the field or in the stadium. On average:

- Two teams,
- Two umpires,
- Two or more coaches and support staff,
- Some selectors,
- Some organisers of the match,
- Some groundsmen.

So, give or take, there are around 40 people in total during a single match, even without spectators. Add spectators, and you might easily have 50–60 people watching your every move. As far as the cricketing people are concerned, you are at least aware of who is who and how they matter in the overall scheme of cricket. But you don't know anything for sure about who the spectators are. They might be people of importance; they might not be. But they are all people with a mouth, a smartphone, and an opinion. This means that there are around 50–60 mouths who can talk about you. Either they can talk positively about you, your conduct, your game, or they can say negative things about you.

Do you see where I am heading with this?

When you are a cricketer in India, you are under a microscope.

Now going forward with our example, what is a good scenario? If all things go in your favour, then people will say positive stuff about you. The Mahoul will be that you are a promising talent, you played well.

And the bad scenario is the exact opposite. You could have given your best, but maybe you showed your anger on the field for a minute, or maybe you reacted with frustration towards a teammate, and now this one thing will be magnified 100x outside. This will set the tone of your 'Mahoul'. People will say, "Oh! That guy is a hot-head. He doesn't seem like a team player." This will keep echoing onto the people who don't even know you. They will begin to form an opinion about you based on your Mahoul.

Unfortunately, for cricketers, your Mahoul will shape the chances you get and the level you reach.

Does that mean I want you to become a 'people-pleaser'? Not at all. We are not here to seek validation; we are to excel in our chosen sport. But we should be constantly aware of how each action on the field and off the field affects our 'Mahoul'.

The funny part is that your skills and your talent as a player will form 50% of your Mahoul; the rest is about your personality, how you behave, and how you carry yourself as a sportsperson.

The good things said about you are tiny sparks that will light the way to your future. But the bad things said about you will spread as quickly as a wildfire.

Your job is not to give anyone a chance to start that wildfire. Now, if you can perform badly in a game, that's totally fine. Not every day in the field is a great day. But you should not react in a way that 50–60 people can go out in the world and talk negatively about you. Since you performed poorly, they are already going to talk negatively about you as a player. Ensure that you don't give them any other negative talking points about your personality, behaviour, or conduct on the field. If this atmosphere, or Mahoul gets to the ears of any potential team owners, selectors or boards, they'll ignore you, and your chance to get selected goes for a toss. There's no coming back for you after that. It will be out of your control rather quickly.

So, take control of your emotions and always react in a dignified and gentlemanly way.

If you are a formidable player, rest assured that your Mahoul is going to be made, and you can't do anything about it. Better a good one made than a bad one. More often than not, it will be a bad one. Who does that? People who don't like you are the loudest ones to make noise about you. They will find the most trivial things about you and go around shouting about it from the rooftops.

I'll elaborate on this with a match scenario. If you bowl two overs in a game, and you give 3 runs in one over and 15 runs in the second, more often than not, people will talk about the second over. Always remember that there are people who'd rather talk about your failures than successes. They would rather celebrate you tripping over than helping you stand up. These are the loudmouths who can control your Mahoul.

Look at Hardik Pandya, for example. He plays for India and has taken his team to an IPL victory, yet he has a very negative Mahoul. It may be because of his antics on and off the field, but he has truly achieved great feats in the game of cricket. He has won laurels for the country, but people still booed him to the extent that he broke down inconsolably after winning the T20 World Cup. Whatever he does, maybe something really minuscule, but it gets the ire of big names in the game of cricket.

In your sporting career, there will be people who don't like you, those who see you as competition and want to eliminate you from the race, or people who simply like to gossip. At the end of the day, they're all just humans who like to focus their laser-sharp attention on your shortcomings.

Even players like the great King Kohli or Rohit Hitman Sharma are not oblivious to their Mahoul being created. Social media has amplified this maybe tenfold in the last few years. You can't do anything about it.

Look at Ruturaj Gaekwad. He is a great talent, being mentored for CSK by none other than MS Dhoni. He has performed well time and again in international matches whenever he was given the opportunity. Yet, the Mahoul never seems to pick up in his favour. There is such minimal talk about him that he is never on the BCCI's priority list for the Indian National Team.

Like always, there are some exceptions to a negative Mahoul being created. It's purely their luck. Rohit Sharma is such an exception. Rohit Sharma's Mahoul was super positive from day one. Even before he entered the National Team, people spoke about this talented lad who showed promise. Mind you, there is no doubt here about Rohit's talent, but he was not the amazing player he is today when he started off. Back then, he struggled a lot in different batting positions until he found his rhythm as the opener of the Indian squad. His Mahoul helped him gain more opportunities and cement a position in the National Team.

We can hope to be exceptions like Rohit Sharma, but let's be practical. There is a very minuscule possibility that we might actually be that anomaly. What should you do then?

All you can do to get ahead of this situation is to turn the Mahoul in your favour. Here's how you can do that:

- *Maintain Composure:* Always keep your body language and reactions in check, both on and off the field. Stay composed, even under pressure, and avoid letting your emotions take over.

- *Stay Aware:* Act as if you're always being observed. Whether it's fans, teammates, or the media, remember that your actions are constantly under scrutiny, so respond with care and responsibility.

- *Be Responsible:* Monitor your behaviour and avoid careless actions that can harm your reputation. Consistency in positive conduct builds trust and respect.

- *Network Wisely:* Build a strong network of people who can vouch for your character. Your reputation often depends on how others perceive your conduct and how you communicate with them.

- *Learn from Others:* Pay attention to the mistakes of others and take lessons from them. Keep your emotions in check to avoid falling into the same traps.

- *Avoid Negative Gossip:* Stay clear of gossip and negative conversations. Be known as someone who uplifts the team environment rather than causing unnecessary trouble or tension.

- *Focus on Positive Conduct:* Remember that the way you treat others will eventually reflect back on you. Conduct yourself with integrity and professionalism, both in private and in public.

The simple funda here is to keep calm and kaam se kaam. It will help you in the long run. A good Mahoul can prolong your career and will help overlook your underperforming times. You'll get more chances to make your career and also help you in being in the good books of people who matter.

I want to add a little here about the things I've observed in recent years. Earlier, your Mahoul happened very organically. In today's day and age, however, it can be manufactured. With the right PR and social media teams, many cricketers have made efforts to manufacture a positive Mahoul about them. To a certain extent, it works, but remember, if your talent and skills cannot live up to the fake hype, then all of this Mahoul will crumble in a minute.

Mahoul is a very fickle mistress. One moment, she is on your side, and in another instant, she will turn the tide against you.

Sometimes, a good Mahoul can turn bad pretty quickly if you don't keep your head down and work. If you start taking things for granted, you will pay the price of a negative Mahoul. A prime example of this is Prithvi Shaw. He won the U-19 World Cup and was touted to be one of the best players in his generation, and ready to take the baton from the seniors of the game, but his positive Mahoul turned sour quickly. You should think about who is responsible for that. Some news articles here and there, some people talking here and there, and poof! It's gone. And with this, his performance dipped, and now he has to work extremely hard to bring himself back into the mix because the game waits for no one.

Mahoul is a very powerful thing; it can make a bad patch seem shorter or longer, depending on what people's perception is about you. If people have a positive attitude about you, then you'll have more cheerleaders. If Mahoul had already been negative about you, then this bad patch would have seemed unending and tedious. Trust me, when you go through a bad form as a player, you don't want the additional pressure of negative things being said about you by anyone and everyone. You want a bigger support system and fewer naysayers on your side!

Does this mean that if you make some mistakes in your career and receive some setbacks, your Mahoul will be negative forever? Not necessarily. Look at Virat Kohli. At one point in his career, he was famous for his foul mouth, his overpowering intensity in games and his anger. Although he has always been talented and hardworking, his Mahoul did become negative to the point where he had to take a step back in his career. But with a conscious shift in mindset, conduct, and communication, he made a comeback like no other. Today, we see a mature Kohli on the field, who radiates positivity and love for the game. This Kohli rebuilt his image with the same hard work that he puts into his batting!

The moral here is to never lose hope. If you've made mistakes in your journey, it's okay. Don't be too harsh on yourself. Take a deep breath, assess where you are, and restart with a fresh mind.

Your Mahoul is going to be a by-product of your personality. If you build a personality that is professional, positive, and well-balanced, your Mahoul is bound to be positive.

We've all read the sticker, 'Smile! You're on camera' wherever there are CCTV cameras installed in public spaces. Make this your mantra for your Mahoul. Remember, someone's always watching, so you better put your best foot forward!

Chapter XVIII

Lady Luck

———※※———

"Luck is luck."

Sports are often celebrated as a test of skill, strategy, and endurance. The best athletes train tirelessly to master their craft, sharpening their technique and honing their mental game. Yet, despite all the preparation, discipline, and raw talent, one undeniable truth remains—luck plays a role in sports.

You can deny it all you want, but the harsh truth is that luck is an important factor in the game. You need lady luck to be on your side for that edge to win.

Some games are designed to minimize luck, ensuring that the most skilled individuals or teams rise to the top. Others, however, leave room for unpredictability, where a lucky bounce, an unexpected injury, or even a gust of wind can alter the course of history. This fine balance between skill and chance defines the essence of competition, making victories sweeter and upsets even more exhilarating.

When it comes to cricket, luck plays an even more vital role!

Right from the start of any game, you need luck for the toss to be in your favour. If the toss doesn't go in your favour, then you pray that at least you are lucky enough to get what you want, whether batting or fielding first, as per your plans.

When on the field, you hope that luck favours you, especially with decisions taken by umpire rulings. You need luck to get favourable weather during the game. You need a tiny piece of luck when your edge flies over to third man, and there isn't a fielder there or can't get to the ball in time. Dropped catches and midfields when you're at the crease are pieces of luck that you want. These are just small instances that highlight the importance of luck in cricket.

But these are also instances completely out of your control, as you very well know. ***You can't prepare for luck, you can only hope for it.***

When you are in the right place at the right time, it is called having good luck. Simple.

The Skill vs. Luck Spectrum in Sports

Every sport falls somewhere between two extremes—pure skill and pure luck. On one end, there's something like a mathematics test, where success is entirely based on ability and preparation. On the other, there's rolling dice, where no amount of talent can change the outcome. Most sports sit somewhere in between, with some relying more on skill while others leave more room for randomness.

Take chess, for example. It's a game of complete skill—there are no dice rolls, no referee decisions, no weather conditions affecting the outcome. The better player wins almost every time. Compare that to a game like poker, where even the most skilled player can lose to a beginner if luck is against them in a particular hand.

Why Some Sports Are More Skill-Based

1. More Games, Less Luck

The longer a competition lasts, the more likely it is that skill will shine through. This is why leagues like the NBA (basketball) and MLB (baseball) play long seasons. A single game might have some lucky moments—a last-second buzzer-beater or a fluke home run—but over the course of 82 (NBA) or 162 (MLB) games, the best teams will generally rise to the top. The sheer volume of games smooths out the randomness, making sure that luck plays a smaller role in deciding champions.

2. More Scoring Opportunities

In sports like basketball, teams take dozens of shots every game, and over time, skill wins out. A single lucky three-pointer won't decide a season because the best shooters take enough attempts to prove their superiority. This is also why star players in basketball have such a big influence on the game—their skill directly impacts multiple plays, reducing the impact of random chance.

Why Some Sports Feel More Random

1. Fewer Games, More Surprises

In contrast, sports like football have much shorter seasons. With 38 in European football leagues, a couple of refereeing mistakes, or unlucky injuries can derail an otherwise great team. The shorter the season, the more likely it is that luck will play a major role in shaping outcomes.

2.   Fluid Play and Limited Control

Some sports naturally involve more randomness due to their structure. Ice hockey, for instance, has constant movement, quick possession changes, and low-scoring games. A single lucky deflection or an untimely mistake can be the difference between victory and defeat. Since even the best players can't dominate every moment (they can only be on the ice for limited minutes), the sport naturally lends itself to more unpredictability.

Team vs. Individual Sports

In individual sports, luck plays a smaller role. Tennis, swimming, sprinting—these are contests where an athlete's preparation and execution determine the outcome. That's why legends like Serena Williams, Michael Phelps, and Usain Bolt could dominate for years; there was little that could interfere with their skill translating into victory.

In team sports, however, no single athlete can control everything. Even the best cricketer needs teammates to contribute. A footballer can't single-handedly win a match if their defenders make mistakes. The more players involved, the more variables at play, increasing the role of luck.

Why This Matters

Some fans love the idea of skill determining the best, while others embrace the unpredictability that makes sports thrilling.

- Skill-dominant sports reward consistency. The best teams and players usually win.

- Luck-influenced sports create drama, allowing underdogs a real shot at glory.

Cricket, my sport, sits in an interesting place on this spectrum. Over a long series, skill generally wins out. But in a single match, particularly in T20 cricket, a lucky edge past the stumps, a dropped catch, or even the toss can be decisive. The shorter the format, the bigger Lady Luck's role.

At the highest level, every athlete is skilled. But no matter how prepared you are, sport is unforgiving—sometimes, all it takes is one moment of fortune or misfortune to decide your fate.

So far, I have explained the intangible aspect of luck. Now I am going to explain the mathematics of luck.

THE MATHEMATICS OF LUCK

Lady Luck is fickle, and the magnitude of her fickleness depends on two things:

1. Number of variables in your game
2. Number of games in your championship series

These two factors determine how much of an impact lady luck will have on your sporting career. There are some games where the variables are few:

1. Table tennis
2. Tennis
3. Sprint
4. Swimming
5. Badminton
6. Basketball

There are some sports where the number of variables is higher:

1. Cricket

2. Baseball

However, the highest number of variables is in Cricket. Let me share why:

1. The Toss: The first variable is the toss. Whether the toss or the decision to bat or field first will be in your favour depends on if lady luck favours you.

2. The weather - it affects only sports played outdoors. Cricket is one of them. Additionally, the conditions change during the course of the match, this also impacts your game.

3. The ground conditions vary from stadium to stadium, country to country. Similar to the weather, the ground conditions also keep changing over time during the match.

4. The time of sport, the conditions in the match will vary depending on when the match is played

5. The balls used in the game also face wear and tear during the match. Hence, the condition of the ball will affect your game.

6. Type of match, generally, in all other sports, the format of the game remains the same, except for cricket. We have test matches, ODIs and T20s. The format also plays a role in the game.

All of these variables are unique to the sport of cricket. In other sports, the variables are much lower and can most likely be overcome with skill and hard work. But in cricket, you have to constantly strategise and execute based on the variables.

The next aspect is the number of games in the championship series. The fewer the number of games in a championship, the higher the luck factor.

Michael Mauboussin, the author of 'The Success Equation', has analysed different sports on the scale of luck to skill, where the game of Roulette is most luck-dependent and basketball's NBA is the most skill-based. He decoded that games that are more skill-oriented depend on two factors:

1. Number of games

2. Number of chances to score

Due to these two factors, basketball's NBA championship with 82 games and highest chances to score becomes the most skill-oriented game, almost eliminating luck! In a basketball game, every team can strategise their entire gameplay around Kobe Bryant (RIP Legend) or Michael Jordan. They can keep taking shot after shot, increasing their mathematical probability of scoring.

But the same is not true for cricket. You cannot send your star batsman onto the field repeatedly, nor can you keep asking your best bowler to bowl every over.

On football grounds, the Argentinian team can keep passing the ball to Messi, increasing their chances of scoring a goal. All the players in a football match, other than the goalkeeper, have the fluidity to keep moving across the field as and when the conditions demand.

Such fluidity is not afforded to cricket players. The rules allow you to display only one aspect of your game at a time.

The other factor about the number of games in a season is also variable and depends on your Cricket Board and management. Some teams play more games; some play less. Some have more matches at home, and some have more away games. The more matches played, the lesser the effect of luck. The fewer matches played, the more you have to depend on luck. There is no fixed number, and the conditions of each match will vary, too!

Hence, on this scale, from luck to skill, luck holds a higher weight in cricket. This is the logical, mathematical, and, unfortunately, brutal truth!

The Athletes' Perspective on Luck

Now that you have grasped the role luck plays in cricket, I want to ask you this question, What should your attitude be towards 'lady luck'?

Should luck become a deciding factor in all your performances? Should luck be the reason you had a good day or a bad day on the field?

No.

You need to strike a balance between becoming fully superstitious and dependent on luck or ignorant and cynical about its role. You need to have a healthy perspective on luck. An athlete's perspective.

First and foremost, accept the fact that a lot of things are out of your control. The variables are called 'variables' for a reason. You cannot predict them fully. You may be able to narrow down the range in which they will occur, but it cannot be 99.99999% accurate.

The second thing that you must accept is that not every day on the field is going to be 'your day'. Most of the days are going to be bad, and some days are going to be good.

Thirdly, build a strong self-belief in your talent and skills. Also, build a strong self-belief of 'I will be lucky one day'. Learn to respect luck as a force of nature but do not depend on it. Think of Joginder Sharma in the 2007 World T20 finals. He was bowling the crucial last over, and all batsmen were playing on the front foot. He bowled a ball that made Misbah go on the back foot and turn the ball behind where there was only one fielder. The ball went to that fielder, and we won the World Cup! India's first T20i WC. Do you see how luck might favour you on a crucial day? So be prepared for it. Never lose hope.

Most importantly, never make luck your crutch. Never blame only luck for your bad days and failures. Always be introspective about what went wrong and how you could have responded/performed better.

Remember, your luck is most tested right before important matches and tournaments. I have seen players who have suffered random injuries like dislocating their shoulder while wearing a t-shirt right before a selection match. The injuries and how they happen are so illogical and frustrating that it becomes mentally tough to deal with. So, be very careful and vigilant about your surroundings at all times.

Lastly, the day when you feel luck is in your favour. When you feel that everything is aligned just for you, capitalise on it fully. Don't let go of that opportunity. In the ODI World Cup of 2023, Glenn Maxwell vs Afghanistan understood that luck was in his favour when two catches that would have definitely sent him back to the pavilion were dropped early on in the match, and he made the most of it. He played one of his career-best knocks and scored 200 runs for Australia. Whatever ball he hit turned to gold. It was a knock that changed Australia's fortunes in the World Cup.

The moral of the story is that 'fortune favours the bold'. So take control and play your best on that day. If you do that, you will be phenomenal and unstoppable on the field.

Chapter XIX

Play to Learn

"Observant athletes are always two steps ahead."

Every day on the field is a day of privilege for you. You are living your dream, and it is your job to make the most of it.

When I say make the most of it, I don't just mean 'do your best, play to your full potential'. This is a given. But I want you to go beyond that; I want you to develop an attitude of 'Play to Learn'.

This attitude will take you a long way in sports. If you spend every minute on the field with this thought process of constant learning, then you will definitely grow exponentially as a player.

What is the 'Play to Learn' Attitude?

The 'Play to Learn' attitude is the cornerstone for success in your sporting career. The definition of this attitude is straightforward. It can be divided into four powerful steps:

1. Self-Reflection
2. Learning

3. Executing the learning

4. Backing your instincts

With every game you play, if you can follow these steps, you will start building the 'Play to Learn' attitude. The moment you begin looking at every game as a learning experience, you will see a change within yourself. Because if you don't learn, then this journey is useless.

Many players spend years on the field doing the same things, both right and wrong. These are the players who will remain stagnant in their careers. Without self-reflection and without learning, they will literally be the same player at the start of their career and at the end of it. If you don't want to be one of them, then start consciously building the 'Play to Learn' attitude.

In regular 9 to 5 careers, your journey to becoming a stalwart is directly proportional to the number of years you spend in your job role. However, in any kind of sport, this relationship doesn't exist.

There could be players who have spent a decade on the field, but if they haven't performed accordingly, they will never be called 'stalwarts'. And there might be youngsters who have little on-paper experience, but if their performances are exceptional, they will be spoken of as stalwarts of the game.

This parity is only due to the fact that some players are constantly evolving with every match, while some players are just playing the same game, day in and day out.

It is up to you where you see yourself going.

Breakdown of the Play to Learn Attitude

1. **Self-reflection**

   Self-reflection is the act of unbiased introspection. After every game, I want you to take a couple of minutes where you look back at every aspect of your performance in the match, whether it is fielding, batting, or bowling. Look at everything you have done for the day.

   For example:

   - Today, you bowled good yorkers - this is a good thing.
   - You misfielded, and that led to a loss of 4 runs for your team - this is a bad thing.

   List down all the things that went right and all the things that went wrong. Do not try to justify anything; simply let it flow the way it is without judgements and explanations.

2. **Learning**

   When you are equipped with your self-reflection, the next step should be learning. Self-reflection without learning is, once again, a useless activity. Talk to your coach or a senior in the team about your reflections and understand what you should learn from them. If you don't have someone you trust with your experience, then trust your instincts and list out your learning alongside the introspection.

   For example:

   - What did you do for the good yorker? Think of how your run-up was, the action, and the condition of the ball.
   - How did you misfield? Think back to when you misjudged the angle or the trajectory of the ball, or were you slow in the chase, etc.

These learnings will take you one step closer to the 'Play to Learn' attitude.

3. Execution

You've mentally understood what needs to change or what you need to keep doing the same. Now, with the help of visualisation and practice, you have to execute what you have learnt in the next match.

This is probably the toughest part of the 'Play to Learn' attitude process because everything else happens in your head; this is the part that happens on the field practically.

4. Backing your instincts

You may not know this or may have not realised this, but our subconscious mind can differentiate between relevant and irrelevant information in a mere split-second. Our decisions are greatly influenced by our subconscious associations. I've experienced this in real time. Hence, I urge you to back your instincts, both on and off the field. Sometimes, you will fail your instincts, and sometimes, your instincts will fail you, but more often than not, your instincts will take you the right way forward.

On the field, you are going to have to make quick decisions, and for that, you must rely on and back your instincts because your subconscious mind has registered a pattern in its head, which is accurate more often than not. It's like a spider-sense. Respond to it. So, if you feel your opponent is going to go for your backhand while serving, make sure you are ready to move and rip one across to him.

Always Trust Your Instincts

How to channel Play to Learn in Success & failure?

As I have mentioned earlier, it is important to analyse both the good and bad aspects of your performance. This logic is applicable to the overall success or failure of your performance too.

There are going to be good days and bad. Knowing sports, there will be more bad days than good. Your job is to stay balanced in the face of crushing failure and crazy success. This will also come only through conscious practice.

First, when analysing your failure or success, stay neutral and be objective. Don't overthink. Don't let your mind wander down the rabbit hole. Analyse, learn and move on.

Also, as I have said earlier in this book, BE SHAMELESS. Don't let anyone else make you feel like 'it's the end of the world'. Learn to shrug off the failure.

This brings me to another important point – 'Raat gayi, baat gayi'.

Never carry yesterday's problems, analysis, or performance into the next day. Learn to leave it there. Just ask yourself:

"Did I learn something from yesterday?"

If you've answered yes, then it's time to move on positively from that terrible performance.

Come Play to Learn Real Life Examples

Let me take you back to 2001, the Border-Gavaskar Trophy between India and Australia. This series is a matter of prestige for both our Men in Blue and the Aussies. In 2001, India was hosting the Trophy.

Team Australia, led by Steve Waugh, was very confident and champion. The team had outstanding players, namely Adam Gilchrist, Matthew Hayden, Ricky Ponting, Brett Lee, Glenn McGrath, Jason Gillespie, and the mighty Shane Warne. A total star-studded cast it was indeed.

On the other hand, Team India was led by Sourav Ganguly. Our team had the OG greats Sachin Tendulkar, Rahul Dravid, VVS Laxman, Harbhajan Singh, and Zaheer Khan.

In the first match of the series, played in Mumbai, Australia won by ten wickets. They not only won the game but also mentally dominated our players.

The second match of the test series held in Kolkata also began on a rough note for India. The first innings saw a brilliant 97 by Mathew Hayden and a massive total of 445. India made a measly 171 and had to take on a follow-on. At that point, Michael Slater taunted the Indian team with a box of cigars, which the Australian team would open once they had defeated India in the second innings.

It was at this crucial moment that VVS Laxman and Rahul Dravid were at the crease. Together, they batted on Day 3 and Day 4, recording one of the most historic comebacks of all time. VVS posted 281, and Dravid scored 180. Their partnership alone shook the Australian team to its core. Later, Harbhajan Singh came out and destroyed the Aussies with 13 wickets in the match. Matthew Hayden's cigars remained unopened for the entire series as India demolished Australia 2-1.

This tournament and particularly this victory are considered one of the greatest in international test cricket. I have specifically chosen this as the example for 'Play to Learn' because had our players not followed this technique, we would never have made this comeback.

Imagine if our players had only analysed and not learnt or executed what they had learnt in the second match. Or worse, if they had been guilt-ridden over their bad performance, leading to a distraught Team India giving up the trophy to Australia. But we didn't do either. We learnt our lessons and implemented what we learnt in a magnificent manner.

Similarly, look at Team India in the ODI Cricket World Cup of 2023. Under Rohit Sharma's captaincy, we did exceptionally well, except at the finals against Australia. The loss was so heartbreaking that it took months for the average cricket fan to recover. How difficult must it be for the players to recover?

And yet, our men in blue, resilient as ever, kept learning, kept evolving and brought the T20I World Cup home in 2024 under the same captain, nonetheless.

This shows what the 'Play to Learn' attitude can win for you in life.

The Other Ways to Play and Learn:

So far, I have written about how your own game should teach you and help you evolve. But if I were to say that this is the only way in which you will build the 'play to learn' attitude, then I would be limiting your learning to a personal experience.

In fact, I never want you to stop learning. So, my suggestion would be to go ahead and watch the sport with a keen eye. There is always something to learn when you watch it. If you saw Suryakumar Yadav's catch in the 2024 T20I World Cup finals, it was not an easy-breezy catch. It was a catch that has resulted as a culmination of years of fielding training and practice to hold your nerves. If he hadn't held his nerves, then that catch and that match were a goner!

Similarly, watch other sports as well. Watch tennis, watch football, watch badminton and hockey. Keep watching and learning. Every player, every match, is bound to teach you something or the other. Some players like Ronaldo will teach you how to handle pressure, some players like Federer will teach you how to stay graceful even at the peak of success, and some players like Kobe Bryant will teach you how to master your mind and then your game!

Application of Your Learnings

In the breakdown of the 'Play to Learn' process, I have stated that the last step is the execution/application of your learning. This is the most vital step to make this exercise a success. Otherwise, you might end up becoming a procrastinator who only thinks and analyses but does nothing.

As a sportsperson, I don't have the luxury of procrastination. My profession demands action, swift action at all times. So whatever you learn must be applied on the field.

How will you do this?

1. Build a high self-awareness and be vigilant on the field.

2. Whenever you are in a situation that was a part of your analysis and learning process, recognise it immediately.

3. Once you have recognised it, remember what the application is going to be.

4. Maintain a diary of your observations.

5. APPLY INSTANTLY.

When I say maintain a diary of your observations, what do I mean by that? Mentally, when you make notes of any observations, make sure you write them down. Why? Because you are human, and you can forget things. But as an athlete, you can't afford to. Let me explain.

Suppose you bowled a ball, something happened, and the ball went perfectly well. What was it that you did right here? Make a mental note, and then pen it down in your diary so that you can practice this again and again. This is helpful not only for the present but also for future reference. In case you're not getting things right in the future, you can always go back to the diary and rectify your mistake. Also, by the future, I don't mean the next few matches but also for years to come. Why I say this is because as years pass by, you start to develop a few bad habits, which are very natural for an athlete. For example - it can be as minuscule as a slight change in the angle at which your foot lands while bowling. This can change the angle of the delivery completely. At this point, referring to the diary can be of utmost importance

Keep yourself in the driving seat and take action. Sometimes in a team sport it may so happen that there is no possibility for you to take action.

For example, if there is just one over left to defend your team, you can go up to the captain and share your input on what might work in the situation. Your input will help the team to strategise, and this will be a great opportunity for you to apply what you have learnt.

My last piece of advice on this would be never stop playing, never stop learning!

Chapter XX

Stay With the Game

◆❖◆

"Be grateful to your sport.
It was the greatest teacher you did not ask for."

If you are a true professional athlete, it is your moral obligation to give back to the game in whatever capacity you can, regardless of your success or failure in the game. Rather than sulking or boasting about your wins or losses, you should try to make things easier for athletes to come.

If you're wondering how to do this, then let me tell you a few ways you could do it.

1. Find ways to help another athlete, whether it is in the form of coaching or S&C.

2. If you find a young athlete struggling with his or her thoughts, you could try being a mentor, aid in making them focus on the game rather than any worrisome thoughts in the head.

3. Monetary gains are important, but not everything you do is for money.

4. Help athletes understand life outside the game so they don't end up ruining their lives.

5. Find good career options in ancillary activities related to your sport so you have a sense of belonging, and it makes your job easier to give back to the game. For example, a good S&C coach working with athletes will help take the sport forward.

6. You can try becoming a part of the system to improve the system for fellow athletes and observe, help select and pick real talent for the game.

As long as you wish to give back to the sport that you played, love, and cherish, you will always find another way to give back to the sport. After all, the game is bigger than any individual, and just by being a part of it, playing it at whatever level you did, it just adds to your life.

Always remember:

Play Hard, Enjoy the Game, Stay with the Game, and Help the Game.